TOLKIEN
IN PERSPECTIVE

SIFTING THE GOLD
FROM THE GLITTER

**A Look at the
Unsettling Power of
Tolkien's Mythology**

BY

GREG WRIGHT

For the GALBREATHS —

[signature]

EPH. 3:20-21

Published by VMI Publishers,
Sisters, Oregon

incider@hotmail.com

For My Nephews Richard, Jacob, Daniel and Robert:
The Keepers of the Maps

ACKNOWLEDGMENTS

The first and greatest human debt I owe is to David Bruce. Not only did he extend profound trust when inviting me to collaborate on the *Rings* coverage on Hollywood Jesus, he also provided me with brotherly encouragement when I most needed it. If that weren't enough, he then suggested that this book be written.

I also consider my wife, Jenn, a full partner in this work. Her support has not been merely theoretical, but practical in ways both physical and metaphysical.

To Regina Doman and her husband, Andrew Schmiedicke, I am indebted for their patient Christian brotherhood in offering a very learned Catholic perspective on my Protestant American biases.

To my other manuscript readers— Will Drummond and Terry Garvin — I also extend my heartfelt thanks, as I do to my most influential literary mentors: Tom Tangney, Miceal Vaughan and Jane Shore.

Finally, for whatever of worth may be found in this volume, to God be all the glory.

PREFACE

This is a book for people who claim the name of Christ.

I also claim the name of Christ. So did J. R. R. Tolkien, and so also, most likely, do you. So this is what we share, not what distinguishes us — or puts us above criticism. Not everything a Christian thinks or does is sacred.

To me, this assumption is a given. It's therefore not preposterous to presume that any work produced by a self-professed Christian will contain flaws, this book included. No matter how clever or creative we as humans might be, we are doomed to fall short in our efforts to emulate our Creator.

That Tolkien would agree with these sentiments is also to me a given. As one Pulitzer prize-winning writer put it, a human being "cannot be known to another — or to himself."[1] The serious student of Middle-Earth will have absorbed enough of Tolkien's thoughts through studies of his texts, manuscripts and letters to guess, if not explicitly recall, that the creator of Hobbits himself wrote words to that effect.

However, the two years preceding the release of Peter Jackson's version of *The Fellowship of the Ring* for New Line Cinema confirmed that very little in this world should be taken for granted. In particular, my work on Tolkien-related analyses for the cutting-edge cultural barometer called *hollywoodjesus.com* taught me that these assumptions — that Christian artists are not above criticism, and that Tolkien himself would agree — are invalid or irrelevant for many Christian fans of *The Lord of the Rings* and related writings.

Some of my point-and-click critics assumed that their wrath at my supposed ignorance would kindle a similar response on my part. One correspondent went so far as to use Tolkien's own words against me, warning, "Do not meddle in the affairs of wizards, for they are quick to anger." I was mostly just puzzled.

I can safely claim that the coverage of Tolkien's work on *hollywoodjesus.com* drew several million readers during those two years, and the more vocal Christian Tolkien fans who visited the site tended to fall into one of two camps. Either they wholeheartedly endorsed (if badly paraphrased) Tolkien's description of *The Lord of the Rings* as "classically Christian," or they found in Tolkien's fantasy an enemy more potent, perhaps, than Sauron himself. My primary intent during the years leading up to the release of the movie was to contribute at least one voice of moderation amidst the hype and hysteria. I wished to take some of the unnecessary sheen off rabid Tolkien defenders, and to bring a little light into the darkness of fearful detractors. I find it neither necessary to endorse Tolkien's work as "required reading in every Christian household,"[2] as Joseph Pearce puts it, nor condemn it as the work of demons.

Alas, my noble attempts were largely sabotaged by my own inability to foresee that Tolkien fans were neither as likely as I to assume that "Christian" authors are as human as non-Christian writers, nor as likely to appreciate that Tolkien saw the potential for moral error in his own work. This was my fault, of course, not that of the fans.

This book is also for Tolkien fans. I, too, count myself as a fan. This claim is not intended to be patronizing. After all, why would any writer who is *not* a fan of

Tolkien devote a significant chunk of his adult life to the study of such an extensive body of work? Well, there's enjoyment in it, of course. My motives are neither mercenary nor malicious.

Perhaps you might also ask yourself, "Why would any fan so thoroughly hunger and thirst after Middle-Earth to have lost track of the number of times through *The Hobbit, The Lord of the Rings, The Silmarillion, The Tolkien Reader*, and Robert Foster's *A Guide to Middle-Earth;* to have been at least twice through *Unfinished Tales;* and to have dabbled heavily in the multi-volume *History of Middle-Earth*"? We might also ask why a writer like Tolkien would devote better than 50 years to creating and refining a work originally conceived as a self-described "private hobby."[3]

The answer to these questions is the same, and balefully obvious: there is something wholly compelling about Middle-Earth, and the tales that leapt so fully developed from the mind of J. R. R. Tolkien. However, if we are realistic, we must admit that there is much more at work in our relationship with Tolkien's tales than appreciation of a rollicking, frolicsome yarn. What is it, precisely, that's at work? How much is due to Tolkien? How much to God? And how much to our own needs and desires?

As an adolescent, my own obsession with Tolkien drew me into calligraphy and a nine-month project to reproduce, by hand, parchment enlargements of the four maps from *The Hobbit* and *The Lord of the Rings*. Anyone who has ever etched Mirkwood tree by India-inked tree can tell you that this is not "normal" behavior; neither is the behavior of my wife's high school chum who wrote notes to her in Elvish. This is behavior bordering on the truly fanatical.

And if my undergraduate professors found my over-long essays on Tolkien a bit "over the top," what did they make of Tolkien's works themselves? It's fair to say that few writers, if any, have produced a body of fiction as logically consistent as Tolkien's; and because most good writers are a bit unhinged compared to the average reader, what can we make of the mind of the visionary of Middle-Earth?

There is much of a Christian nature which I admire in Tolkien's work. There can be no doubt, as we will see, that these elements are there by design; and what has been given to God cannot be taken away. Yet, as is the case with anything of merit that you or I might do, there is little credit that Tolkien can take for what nuggets of gold may be found: for there is only One who is Good; He is the Way, the Truth, and the Life, and if something of Him can be seen in Tolkien's work it's because Truth can't be hidden. To co-opt Tolkien's own analogy, it is impossible to completely separate the corn from the chaff; but after the job is done, corn is still corn, and the corn is to the credit of the grower not the thresher. Likewise, to give God credit for the beauty and truth found in Tolkien's writing takes nothing away from Tolkien or his work. There is a difference between the corn and the chaff after all; and some threshers do better work than others.

At the same time, because Tolkien is not the Master Refiner Himself, there remains, strewn amidst our Author and Perfector's gold, some of the writer's own personal dross. If we are to be at all honest with ourselves, we must admit that there is a great deal in this world which, to our eye, glitters — and yet which is *not* gold. There may even be those who would elevate *The Lord of the Rings* to the level of Holy Writ, or who might wish to beatify Tolkien. But in our hurry to embrace the beauty and truth that we do find in Tolkien's works, we may find that we have also unwittingly embraced some unsavory deceptions. In our eagerness to consume the True Corn Tolkien threshed into his story, we may rashly consume excessive chaff.

Again, this is not a condemnation of Tolkien; it can only be expected that both he and his "subcreation" are less than perfect. Rather, it is our fault, because we chase after words that would tickle our ears; it is our own desire that leads us astray. The only proof that we, as Christian Tolkien fans, need that this is true is to consider how comparatively much we know about Middle-Earth, and how little about the Kingdom of God.

It is disingenuous to excuse an obsession with Middle-Earth as harmless, merely because it's entertainment, not theology; or because it's much-needed escapism to help us deal with everyday life. By comparison, it is normal and acceptable to appreciate ice cream; it is gluttony to gorge oneself on it. And the reason gluttony is sinful is because hunger for the creation becomes more important than hunger for the Creator.

My aims with this book are twofold: first, to celebrate the corn in Tolkien's threshing, and in so doing help skeptical or critical Christians see how *The Lord of the Rings* can be used to point non-believers to Christ.

By contrast, however, my second aim is to persuade the Tolkien fan that there may be good reasons to maintain a cool relationship with Middle-Earth, and that Middle-Earth may have become more important than God's Kingdom. It would be wise to resist the temptation to delve too deeply, as the Dwarves did in Moria. I hope to persuade the truly fanatic Tolkien devotee that it is time to chain the Balrog. The Book of the 20th century was not *The Lord of the Rings*. It was the Bible: the Book for All Ages, even Tolkien's Fourth Age and beyond.

TABLE OF CONTENTS

Chapter One

MYTH, CULTURE AND CONSECRATION

One of Washington State's more curious news stories of 2002 concerned a roadside marker memorializing the completion of State Route 99. Near the Canadian border some 60 years ago, this road — popularly known as "The Pacific Highway" — was dedicated in honor of Jefferson Davis, President of the Confederacy. It's a little puzzling that a 20th century paved highway in the most remote corner of the contiguous 48 states should come to be named after the most famous of Southern rebels. After all, the boundaries between American and British territories in the Northwest weren't even settled by international mediation until the conclusion of the Pig War of 1872; and statehood didn't come to Washington until 1889.

The heated rhetoric sparked in the state legislature by the recent discovery of the marker, however, served to demonstrate the enduring power of myth in our culture. Myth is, and always has been, as potent as fact. With regard to the Civil War, the myth that the core issue of the war was slavery — so eloquently and convincingly stated by Ken Burns' epic documentary — is essential to a nation that killed hundreds of thousands of its own during the conflict. What better justification could we find than a further broadened definition of "all men," the people to which our Constitution grants rights? Similarly, the myth of Southern independence, restated popularly in Lynyrd Skynyrd's "Sweet Home Alabama" among other places, is necessary to a South that not only suffered the same kinds of human loss as the North, but was also devastated economically. If the South wasn't an integral part of the Union, then what was the fight over?

Yet both myths gloss historic documentation. Many rebel legislators dissented on the general grounds of states' rights, while taking no stand on the specific issue of slavery; at the same time, evidence suggests that the goal of certain Northern political powers was really the economic subjugation of the South. As an economic foe, the South was indeed worthy; yet geographic, economic and political realities still dictate the North's codependent relationship with the South.

Of course, nations (and would-be nations) at times develop their own myths, and the newer and more original the better. Arthurian myth fueled the insistence of the Britons on the right of self rule; the myth of the Noble Savage helped justify French incursions in the New World; the myth of Manifest Destiny goaded our nation's westward expansion; and the myth of Aryan supremacy stoked the furnaces of the Third Reich.

To a certain extent, cultures need myth to survive. The stories we share and tell to one another unite us in common values and purpose. Cultures either resist change because their myths are static; or cultures redirect themselves by deliberately taking charge of their myths.

Where cultural myth is connected to actual historic events, changing the culture and preserving the myth both have their dangers. In a recent episode of *The Education of Max Bickford*, a history professor engages in a bit of historical revisionism in the interests of changing the culture: the actual history of the civil rights movement is transformed into a professor's mythology of personal involvement, in order to shape her students' future. A voice-over expresses one of the lessons the event teaches Bickford's alter ego:

"The past learns lessons from the present."[1] Well, it certainly can if the past is mutable.

John Ronald Reuel Tolkien wished it were, as did many of his fellow British veterans of World War I trench warfare. The ugliness of mechanized war challenged many a man's faith in God and empire. One British gentleman, Jack Hornby, sought to escape the horror of the first "War to End All Wars" through a retreat into the wilds of North America, where, before the war he had been "amiable, gregarious, amenable, gay. Suddenly he had become solitary, resentful, inscrutable, defensively reticent and ironic." The war had merely confirmed "his conviction that civilisation was evil and social man diseased. Yet even when he had placed the length of the Mackenzie River and the breadth of the Great Bear Lake between himself and civilisation he had found fresh bitterness and a most profound desolation."[2]

Meanwhile, Wilfred Owen, the British poet, found an outlet for the passion of his tortured soul through the use of religio-mythic symbolism in his work. Though he had claimed in letters to have suffered a "lapse from the Christian faith,"[3] the enduring force of his work is largely due to his daring use of the very myths he rejected. His reworking of the Abraham / Isaac story to serve as an indictment for the loss of an entire generation of young men, "The Parable of the Old Man and The Young,"[4] is one of the most eloquent anti-war statements of the 20th century.

The same environment which embittered Hornby's experience in the Barrens and left Owen dying in a ditch in France also shaped the young J. R. R. Tolkien. Given to melancholy since the early death of his devoted mother, Tolkien retreated to his pre-war love of language as an outlet for his passion. While moral outrage drove Owen,

Siegfried Sassoon and other artists, Tolkien's passion was typified by a sense of loss and nostalgia: an intense longing for a time when the British myth of God-and-empire still made sense. Pondering the "good, evil, fair, foul" of his war experience directly brought about the mythic back-story to the War of the Ring;[5] and the events of World War II, as he was completing his drafts of *The Lord of the Rings*, only deepened his feeling that "there seem no bowels of mercy or compassion, no imagination, left in this dark diabolical hour."[6] In part, Tolkien's work was an attempt to give meaning to this immediate darkness. Tolkien once explicitly stated that one of the primary objectives of his work was to develop a meaningful mythology for England.[7] Why?

In the modern world, the casting of myths seems a terribly outmoded means of directing social change: witness the pragmatism of the nonviolent resistance movements of the 20th century. Isn't rational action preferable? Can't change be motivated by real need, instead of fueled by manipulative dreams? Why bother to view history, the present and the future through the lens of myths?

As those who claim to represent Christ, we would be wise to first acknowledge the Scriptural precedent for the usefulness of myth. Then we may be equipped to dissect our cultural myths and analyze them against the teachings of Scripture and appreciate why we are so drawn to and motivated by certain myths, and yet are repelled by others. In particular, we may learn why the writings of   J. R. R. Tolkien are remarkably potent for some and so distasteful to many.

Before looking at the general issue of myth in contemporary culture, then, we shall briefly review three passages of Scripture — the Pentateuch, Chronicles and the Gospel of John — to see how Biblical writers, guided by the

Holy Spirit to address specific purposes, approached and recorded historical events.

MYTH AND BIBLICAL WRITERS

"Myth" can be a frightening word. As children, we were taught to think of Scripture as "Truth," and the seminal stories of pagan cultures as "legends" or "myths." Hence, the corpus of ancient Greek legend was commonly labeled "mythology" while the Old and New Testaments of the Bible were exempt from such (supposed) belittlement. The first time that some college professor or enlightened cousin referred to the story of Jesus as a "myth," we either felt outrage or profound confusion.

We should not, of course, exclude the role of Bible-as-myth from the role of Bible-as-revelation because the two are not incompatible. One might say that it is the very nature of the Biblical myths as revelation which elevates them to Scripture: the Spirit-breathed power of God to bring about salvation. The gospel of Jesus Christ is not, and cannot be, contained in any other mythology. We may catch glimpses of the gospel truth in other stories — foreshadowing, even unlooked-for prophecies — but they are glimpses only. The leaves on the ground tell us that a tree is somewhere nearby; but the leaves are not the tree itself.

The word "myth," unfortunately, has acquired a less-than-complimentary, pejorative sense amongst Christians. In reality, however, we find that there is no convenient boundary between myth and history, much as religious conservatives and radical atheists alike would prefer there to be. Periodically, a mythic Troy is discovered to have basis in historic fact; but just as frequently an historian will assert, like Herodotus, that in India we may find gold-digging ants the size of small dogs.[8] "Myth" as it turns out, is defined neither as "fact" or "fantasy," but as "a traditional story of unknown authorship, ostensibly with a historical basis, but serving usually to explain some phenomenon of nature, the origin of man, or the customs, institutions, religious rites, etc., of a people."[9]

There are secondary definitions for "myth" which include descriptors such as "imaginary" and "fictitious"; but these are vernacular usages, not scholarly or academic. In discussion of Tolkien's work as "myth," and in general academia, the definition of the word as given above is operational, and will be used in this book to compare various cultural myths.

Should application of the word "myth" to Scripture, then, be offensive? Only if one chooses to be so offended. The definition is certainly not derogatory in relation to the issue of "purpose." We can clearly state that the Bible exists in part to explain the origin of man, and the customs, institutions and religious rites of Christianity. Offense can only be taken, then, with regards to the issue of "unknown" authorship and an ostensibly ("apparent, seeming, professed"[10]) historical basis.

Moses And The Pentateuch

The first five books of the Bible — collectively referred to as the Pentateuch, and forming the basis of the religious writings of Christianity, Judaism and Islam — have traditionally been understood as penned by the prophet Moses, and his successor Joshua. Moses himself, however (presuming the claim to authorship is authentic), does not identify the source of the many stories which make up Genesis, the first of the five books. Moreover, Moses is not in the least concerned with historical corroboration. He is entirely content to leave the origin of his stories unknown, and to rely on a mere profession of the historic basis for his account. It is doubtful that Moses would quibble with the classification of much of his work as pure myth.

Why? Because Moses did not himself understand his writings as history. For him, and for his audience, there was much more at stake — clarifying for the Israelites why they were unique, *qodesh*, holy, set apart. In purely rational terms, this mythic clarification would have been simple to summarize: "We, the people of Israel, are unique because we have been created by a God who is Himself holy, and we have been created in His image. Further, we, amongst all the other peoples of the earth, have been chosen by Him to bring great blessing to the world, because of the faithfulness of our fathers. God has continually confirmed this special relationship with us in powerful and miraculous ways, not the least of which was our deliverance from Egypt. Nonetheless, we are a stubborn and arrogant people, so God has need to provide the means to restore us to a right relationship to Him, through His Law."

Again, Genesis is "mythic" not because it is *untruthful;* it is mythic because it professes to have basis in historic fact *without concern for historic authentication.* Genesis is wholly lacking in the kind of corroboration one may find in other books of the Old Testament, such as Daniel or 1 and 2 Kings. There are no references to external, pre-existing documents; there is no attempt to correlate time periods or characters with Egyptian or Chaldean chronologies and histories; and there is an almost confounding obsession with an internal geographical frame of reference which is by nature wholly unverifiable: the antediluvean Four Rivers of Eden.

For Moses and his followers, the power of Genesis lay not in the idea that it was good *history*, but that it was *good* history: that is, a history which was useful and instructive *for them*, if for no one else. The Genesis story of creation does not provide details in a fashion which would satisfy intelligent design advocates or evolution theorists; but *was* told in a manner which confirmed the individuality and power of God, and His unique and special relationship with man. How much use, after all, would the average sixth-century B.C. Hebrew have had for an intelligent design vs. evolution debate? The book of Genesis as written would be of great use, however, in helping to sort out the religious dilemmas of the early Israelite's day. Today, we might be hard pressed to choose between Sprint, MCI, or AT&T. In Joshua's day, the choices were Dagon, Molech, Ashtoreth or God.

Having established in Genesis why this People was chosen by God to be delivered from Egypt, Moses moves on in Exodus, Leviticus and Numbers to answer the second significant identity question for Israel: where does their tradition as a nomadic people come from, and why? Historians may gripe that Moses' account lacks the necessary details to sort out the logistical support and geographical movement necessary to shepherd two or three million people around the Sinai Peninsula. They may also point out that Exodus is less than definite about the naming and location of God's holy mountain. But again, Moses did not write these accounts as travel guides for Sinai. Rather, he wrote to remind the people of Israel that they were stubborn; that their fate was ultimately in God's merciful hands; and that even their leaders were subject to great moral failure.

In setting down the details of God's detailed laws in Deuteronomy — the fifth and final book of the Pentateuch which contains the eloquent "blessing and curse" passages — Moses was careful to tie stipulations of The Law to the subjectively told, ostensibly historical stories selected for inclusion in the earlier books. So when the children of Israel ask, "Father, why do we celebrate the Feast of

Tabernacles?" their fathers do not reply, "I don't know; it's just history." Rather, they tell their children, "All native-born Israelites are to live in booths so your descendants will know that I had the Israelites live in booths when I brought them out of Egypt. I am the LORD your God."[11] When they ask why they are taught to be kind to strangers, they are told "Why, we ourselves were strangers in Egypt once,"[12] and when the children ask why they observe the Passover, the ritual itself provides the answer: "Observe the month of Abib and celebrate the Passover of the LORD your God, because in the month of Abib He brought you out of Egypt by night. Sacrifice as the Passover to the LORD your God an animal from your flock or herd at the place the LORD will choose as a dwelling for His Name. Do not eat it with bread made with yeast, but for seven days eat unleavened bread, the bread of affliction, because you left Egypt in haste — so that all the days of your life you may remember the time of your departure from Egypt."[13]

> "So Moses wrote down this law and gave it to the priests, the sons of Levi, who carried the ark of the covenant of the LORD, and to all the elders of Israel. Then Moses commanded them: 'At the end of every seven years, in the year for canceling debts, during the Feast of Tabernacles, when all Israel comes to appear before the LORD your God at the place he will choose, you shall read this law before them in their hearing. Assemble the people — men, women and children, and the aliens living in your towns — so they can listen and learn to fear the LORD your God and follow carefully all the words of this law. Their children, who do not know this law, must hear it and learn to fear the LORD your God as long as you live in the land you are crossing the Jordan to possess.'"[14]

So we find that the Pentateuch is much more important to the people of Israel than a mere history could ever have been. Moses did not write history, he employed history: he gleaned stories of his people's past and repackaged them in a way that made them both consumable and meaningful. It was not so important *who* believed the story; but it was crucial who *believed* the story. Similarly, the historic facts of Agincourt may be of academic interest to me; but to this day there are those for whom Agincourt is much more meaningful than mere history. What we believe becomes transformational when it is powerful enough to affect our behavior.

The Shorter History of Chronicles

Was the Pentateuch powerful enough to be transformational for the people of Israel? Yes and no. As a people, Israel still exists and is radically set apart by Torah; yet the book of Judges documents the dismal failure of ancient Israel to complete the work begun under Joshua, because "Israel had no king; everyone did as he saw fit."[15] While providing a historical account of the Davidic dynasty, Samuel, Kings and Chronicles also document that the requirements of the law were never fully implemented under David. Even Solomon, though wise, was still foolish enough to ignore provisions under the law that Israel's king

> "must not acquire great numbers of horses for himself or make the people return to Egypt to get more of them, for the LORD has told you, 'You are not to go back that way again.' He must not take many wives, or his heart will be led astray. He must not accumulate large amounts of silver and gold. When he takes the throne of his kingdom, he is to write for himself on a scroll a copy of this law, taken from that of the priests, who are Levites."[16]

Presumably, if Solomon had actually taken this injunction seriously and written out a copy of Deuteronomy for himself, he never would have become famous for his wives and concubines, his vast stables of Egyptian horses at Megiddo, and his vast wealth. And quite probably, God would not have seen the need to chasten Solomon by turning the kingdom over to Jeroboam. Instead, the struggle between the usurper and Rehoboam divided the kingdom, and by Josiah's time, Judah's priests had all but forgotten Moses' prodigious work.

Contemporary Christians too easily connect Solomon's material blessings with his wisdom and faithfulness. An analysis of the mythic purposes of the writing of both Kings and Chronicles demonstrates that the writers and audience alike were only too painfully aware that Solomon's wisdom was doomed. The demise of Israel was directly linked to Solomon's disobedience of God's laws. The writer, or writers, of Samuel and Kings are intent on detailing the moral failures of Saul, David and Solomon as background to, and precedent for, the prolonged cyclic moral failures which would characterize the leaders of a divided Israel. These books provide object lessons in the history of Israel's leadership, including full exposition of the many pitfalls.

In comparing Chronicles with Samuel and Kings, however, we clearly see the difference between nominally objective history and subjective myth-making. While Chronicles covers the same time period as Samuel and Kings, the writer — and God — has something different in mind: defining for Israel's faithful who "the remnant" are; what their providential purpose is; and what it is that makes them *qodesh qodesh*, Most Holy: further set apart from among the children of Jacob.

Because Chronicles is about the people's identity

rather than the faults of their leadership, the writer's version of history is notably different. Quite noticeably, for instance, the prophet Samuel fades into the background. The moral failures of the kings are also less prominently featured — David's affair with Bathsheba is wholly missing; there is no mention of Absalom's rebellion; and there is only a brief explanation for God's unhappiness with Solomon. Further, the author makes no attempt to track the succession of the kings of Israel. Instead, the first nine chapters deal exclusively with genealogical issues. Chronicles answers these questions: how has the remnant come to find its way back to Jerusalem, and what is the remnant's relationship to the patriarchs and to God?

The focus of their identity is the temple, built by Solomon and rebuilt by the remnant which returned from captivity. A linguistic clue is the abundant use of the term *show'er* in Chronicles: the gatekeeper. The authorship of Chronicles has traditionally been ascribed to Ezra, the priest repatriated to Judea in order to supervise reconstruction of the temple. The importance of the gatekeeper in Chronicles is certainly consistent with the emphasis in Ezra and Nehemiah, which are the only other Old Testament books to make extensive use of *show'er*. The purpose of the gatekeeper? To prevent the unclean from entering the temple, and to guard the temple storehouse. It is from Ezra's revisionist myth-making that Jews — and, later, followers of Christ — would develop the idea of God's people as a figurative temple. Ezra "was inspired of God to write these books to encourage the exilic and postexilic Israelites of his day to build God's house and to center their lives around the worship of God as the only way to survive and to fulfill their destiny."[17] The subtitle of Chronicles could well be, "The Most Holy Place: What People Worship There; Why They Worship, and Why They Must Stay Pure." In Chronicles, it is no longer enough that Israel be God's chosen people; God has mercifully chosen a remnant to maintain the sanctity of His temple.

As with the Pentateuch, we find that Chronicles is much more important to the remnant of Israel than the history of Samuel and Kings on its own could have been. Ezra, like Moses, used history selectively, repackaging it to make it both consumable and filled with meaning specific to the remnant of Israel. It was not so important that *others* believe the story; but it was crucial that the remnant *believed* the story.

The Unique Gospel of John

So was the myth of the remnant powerful enough to be transformational? Again, yes and no. After their return from exile, the Jews managed to avoid replicating many of their ancestors' pitfalls: idol worship, lapses in religious observances, neglect of widows and orphans, and so on. But a new temple and reformed Levitical practice were not sufficient to usher in the Kingdom of God. In fact, as the Pharisee Saul was later to deduce during his sojourn as the Apostle Paul, God had something entirely different in mind with respect to the remnant: a spiritual remnant which forms the basis of the spiritual Israel, ushering in God's Kingdom on earth:

> "I ask then: Did God reject his people? By no means! I am an Israelite myself, a descendant of Abraham, from the tribe of Benjamin. God did not reject his people, whom he foreknew. Don't you know what the Scripture says in the passage about Elijah — how he appealed to God against Israel: 'Lord, they have killed your prophets and torn down your altars; I am the only one left, and they are trying to kill me'? And what was God's answer to him? 'I have reserved for myself seven thousand who have not bowed the knee to Baal.' So too, at the

present time there is a remnant chosen by grace. And if by grace, then it is no longer by works; if it were, grace would no longer be grace. What then? What Israel sought so earnestly it did not obtain, but the elect did. The others were hardened, as it is written: 'God gave them a spirit of stupor, eyes so that they could not see and ears so that they could not hear, to this very day.'"18

And so we find that God's people, His "remnant chosen by grace," are not the physical people of Israel at all, but a "chosen people, a royal priesthood, a holy nation, a people belonging to God," as Peter puts it. "Once you were not a people, but now you are the people of God; once you had not received mercy, but now you have received mercy."19

And who is Peter's audience? "You who believe," he says. Those who claim Christ, the apostles declare, have supplanted Ezra's remnant as gatekeepers of God's temple. Instead, Peter asserts, those who believe, "like living stones, are being built into a spiritual house to be a holy priesthood."20

This spiritual remnant, the elect, was initially limited. As a necessary component to facilitate its growth, the remnant needed its own codified, formalized story of identity: defining who the "spiritual remnant" are; what their providential purpose is; and what it is that makes them further set apart from the physical Israel.

While the synoptic gospels (Matthew, Mark and Luke) all satisfy this objective in declaring the Good News of Jesus as the Messiah, John is the most direct in stating this purpose:

> "Jesus did many other miraculous signs in the presence of his disciples, which are not recorded in this

book. But these are written that you may believe that Jesus is the Christ, the Son of God, and that by believing you may have life in his name."[21]

And so, like Moses and Ezra before him, John used history selectively, repackaging it to make it both consumable and meaningful to the spiritual remnant. And like the original audiences of the Pentateuch and Chronicles, the central issue with John's audience is *belief.*

Data, when used poorly, can be dangerous and misleading; but the importance of the issue of belief to John can be demonstrated by his frequent and consistent use of the term. Of the 136 times that various conjugations of the Greek *pisteuo* — to believe — appear in the Gospels, Matthew contains 11, Mark 15, and Luke ten; startlingly, John contains *the remaining 100.* And so, in John's telling of the story, belief becomes the key factor in defining the remnant, those who have "become children of God — children born not of natural descent, nor of human decision or a husband's will, but born of God."[22]

It is important to note, however, that John's aim is unlike Luke's: he is not primarily interested in "carefully investigating everything" in order to produce "an orderly account."[23] And so there is much in the synoptic accounts which is missing from John (of significant note being the bulk of Jesus' recorded figurative teachings, or "parables"); but at the same time John relates many miracles and events missing from the Synoptics. John does not bother to "document his sources," and while it may be attractive to believe that he himself provided all of the eyewitness accounts for what he wrote, it is not only unlikely but impossible. Who supplied John with the words exchanged between Pilate and Jesus, for instance? And why does John neglect to document such sources? Because John "wrote primarily to convince, not to record facts."[24] Further, he knew that the power to convince lay not in the facts themselves, but in the spiritual power behind those facts; and that, ultimately, belief was an issue of the heart, not the mind.

So in the Gospel of John, we find a collection of stories of indefinite earthly origin, ostensibly with (but not preoccupied with providing) a historical basis, serving the purpose of defining the identity of God's chosen people. By the accepted, conventional academic definition of the word, we have myth.

MYTH AND SCRIPTURE

Again, we may recoil instinctively from such a statement. But as we have seen, it is the Bible's *inspired* nature, not its *mythic* nature, which raises it to the status of Scripture. We may still chafe, however, under the assertion that the Bible can be both truth and myth at the same time. But if we are to apprehend Tolkien at all, it is imperative that we come to grips with the concept, for it was fundamental, as we shall see, to *his* understanding of Scripture.

Further, John's gospel is a myth which falls in a contiguous tradition stretching back through the prophets to Moses himself. And it sees no need to apologize for itself as myth. In fact, the Gospel of John seemingly prides itself in recognizing that a selective, subjective assertion of the person of the Christ will be just as effective a path to faith as Luke's more structured, factual approach. Why? Because the writers of Scripture were inspired by the Holy Spirit; and God has always known that man is rarely moved to action by mere intellectual assent to demonstrable facts. Rather, man consistently acts on faith, often in the face of contradictory facts.

So there is no reason to be offended by the application of the term "myth" to Scripture. In no way does it diminish or denigrate Scripture. God may accomplish his purposes through mythic means as well as any other. And such a realization is particularly useful when considering J. R. R. Tolkien, who had an immense respect for myth. He himself applied the concept to the gospel in a fashion which some might find even more offensive. "I do not mean," he wrote, "that the Gospels tell what is *only* a fairy-story; but I do mean very strongly that they do tell a fairy-story: the greatest."[25] For Tolkien, this was not criticism; it was praise, and must be understood as such.

Yet, much as we must be conscious of the danger of drowning in even a cup of water, we must also be cognizant of the potential dangers of myth. For if we, as those who claim the name of Christ, are truly defined by the myth of the gospel, we must be cautious about embracing competing myths that try to tell us something different about our identity. As Tolkien said, myth can "be carried to excess. It can be ill done. It can be put to evil uses. It may even delude the minds out of which it came."[26] So a close examination of any such myths and works of art is warranted. But before moving on to an analysis of Tolkien and *The Lord of the Rings*, we shall first examine a model for spiritual analyses of art and its artifacts within contemporary culture; then we shall briefly apply the model to a myth perhaps more familiar — *Star Wars* — as a short case study.

A MODEL FOR MYTHIC ANALYSIS

Easy answers are always terribly appealing, but are hard to find. Many people came to Jesus seeking easy answers, and no one ever found one. Think of Nicodemus, approaching Jesus on the Pharisees' behalf, seeking physical evidence of the Messiah. Instead he was given seemingly cryptic words about spiritual rebirth. Think of Mary and Martha sending for Jesus during their brother's dire illness, only to have Jesus wait until after Lazarus' death for

His visit to Bethany. Or think of the rich young man looking for a cookbook approach to righteousness, only to have Jesus pinpoint a unique spiritual weakness. The search for easy answers is ill-motivated, driven by a desire for an end to personal trouble, or as a means of self-justification.

So instead of easy solutions for dealing with spirituality in cultural myths, perhaps we should instead look for difficult answers. Jesus supplied many of these during his earthly ministry. For instance: how did Jesus deal with His disciples' questions about who is "on our side"? On one occasion, the disciples informed Jesus that they had directed a man to stop casting out demons in Jesus' name because the man was not one of Jesus' formal disciples. Jesus' response indicated that the "team" was a lot bigger than the disciples thought: "Do not stop him; for whoever is not against us is for us."[27] That is, "He may not have received his commission directly from me, but he is still honoring me through what he is doing; leave him alone." Yet on another occasion, when the Pharisees accused Jesus of casting out demons by the power of Satan, Jesus declared, perhaps more famously, "He who is not with me is against me." [28]

There's a seeming paradox in the two statements. Applying conventional logic to Jesus' latter words, we could say:

> *if one who is "not with" me is "against" me,*
>
> *then (by negating both halves of the proposition)*
>
> *one who is "with" me is "not against" me.*

(Corollary 1)

So far so good. By applying this corollary to Jesus' prior statement, we can deduce that:

> *if one who is "not against" me is "for" me; and*

> *one who is "with" me is "not against" me*
> (Corollary 1, above)*;*
>
> *then whoever is "with" me is "for" me, and vice versa.*

Seeming paradox resolved.

Or is it? Such an understanding, though it seems logically consistent, tautologically ignores the fact that Judas, who was "with" Christ, was apparently not "for" him. This understanding also defeats the intent of Jesus' teaching in both instances: in the former, Jesus was trying get the disciples not to be so narrow-minded about how ministry was accomplished (celebrating diversity, as a politically-correct person might say today); and in the latter, Jesus was pointing toward homogeneity of purpose. How does one celebrate both diversity and uniformity at the same time?

Consecration and Intent

The answer lies neither in logic nor in political correctness, but in understanding the issue of consecration: there's casting out demons, and then there's casting out demons, as it were. It all boils down to intent, because any judgment of effect can be terribly subjective, even when it comes to the casting out of demons.

To clarify, let's examine a simple, familiar scenario: boys and girls on Valentine's Day. Tommy has a crush on Sue. Sue has a crush on Tommy; but Betty has a crush on Tommy, too. None of the three have articulated their feelings for one another, but each anticipates the evidence of Valentine's Day. Wanting to please Sue, Tommy gives Sue a valentine, but doesn't give one to Betty. Both Betty and Sue give valentines to Tommy. Tommy is happy. Sue is happy, and Betty is crushed. Tommy may have no idea that Betty has been hurt.

Is the giving of valentines inherently good? If so, how can a person possibly be hurt by another person doing something inherently good? Since Betty has been hurt by Valentine's Day, can we conclude that it must be outlawed? The giving of valentines is, of course, neither inherently good nor worthy of banning. Tommy's act is only "good" because it was intended to please Sue. It has been consecrated to Sue, and cannot be made "bad" because of Betty's disappointment. (Naturally, if Tommy only sent Sue a valentine in order to make Betty angry, the act would be "bad.") What is "bad" is, dare we say it of mere children, a selfish reaction on Betty's part. As adults we know that, if Betty really cared for Tommy, she would be happy that Tommy is happy, regardless of the source of that happiness. Betty's happiness is instead contingent only on satisfaction of her own desires, not the satisfaction of the desires of others.

Consecration and Effect

Now, back to our Scriptural example: isn't the casting out of demons unilaterally good? Well, generally speaking, the casting out of demons is "good" because it has been consecrated to God for the glorification of Jesus' name. As Jesus explains, that is the only way an attempt to cast out demons *can* be effective. Yet there were "negative" consequences to the casting out of demons: a fellow-believer, doing what he believed right, had been reprimanded by the narrow-minded disciples; the disciples themselves had been offended by their presumptuous counterpart; and the Pharisees had been scandalized by Jesus' entire ministry. Shall we then declare a moratorium on the casting out of demons?

Not at all. An act consecrated by devotion to Christ, and therefore under jurisdiction of His judgment alone, may still be useless or scandalous. If useless or ineffective, the act is still not damnable; and if scandalous or offensive, the fault likely lies with the one scandalized or offended, not the actor.

As Paul points out to Timothy, "nothing is to be rejected if it is received with thanksgiving, because it is consecrated by the word of God and prayer."[29] In the words of Jesus, it is "the altar that sanctifies the gift."[30] That is, "when the cause is God's, the gift is consecrated."[31] So it is God's judgment, in His omniscience, that will determine whether the gift (or act) has been honored, not our frail human judgment, or our ability to judge fruit.

And so what we might call Consecration Analysis will focus not on effects, but on intent: specifically, has the subject of discussion been consecrated for the glory and honor of God? Or has it instead been consecrated to ego, personal status, glorification of some doctrine of men, or specifically to an attempt to tear down faith? If an act or work has been consecrated to God, we should endeavor to understand how God may be glorified through the subject of analysis, leaving aside any pretense of ability to judge what is strictly between another person and God. If, on the other hand, the act or artifact has been consecrated to other ends, it is incumbent upon us to demonstrate clearly how the work's aims are, in effect, idolatrous, in that the author has put some other agenda before God's. And in either case, it still behooves us, without passing judgment, to identify potential dangers.

Effects analysis, by contrast, would ask as a starting place such questions as: "How are people being led astray?" These avenues of inquiry are fruitless, since all worldly things, even food and sex, can either be used constructively or, through the work of the Accuser, destructively. Even the

Word of God itself has been used over the ages to lead people astray. Shall we condemn the Bible because Nazi Germany, for only one example, was able to twist it to their ends? Indeed not. As novelist Booth Tarkington put it, "To any reader a book is what he brings to it."[32]

The aim of Consecration Analysis, by contrast, is to determine the intent of the author of a work or artistic "act," both through an examination of the evidence within the act itself, and an examination of the claims of its author. Granted, this approach is fraught with peril; but it may prove, through application, to be more objective than anecdotal cause-and-effect empiricism. And we may find that Consecration Analysis, an approach perhaps familiar to students of Aquinas, provides a meaningful framework for directing cultural artifacts toward the glorification of God.

STAR WARS: LATE 20th-CENTURY AMERICAN MYTH

As with *The Lord of the Rings*, those who claim the name of Christ should be intrigued by an analysis of the spirituality in *Star Wars*. "I realized that I had to take it seriously," says journalist Bill Moyers, "because my kids were taking it seriously."[33]

The mind which most influenced George Lucas in the creation of the *Star Wars* film saga was Joseph Campbell's. In his ground-breaking 1949 work, *The Hero With a Thousand Faces*, Campbell coined the term "monomyth,"[34] giving the rationality- and efficiency-minded modern age a way to understand the ways in which myth has always shaped perception, and allowed cultures and peoples to relate to and understand the world. It was no accident, perhaps, that *Star Wars* hit cinematic paydirt.

If the movie had been poorly made, badly acted, and

scored by Weird Al Yankovic instead of John Williams it would have bombed regardless of its cultural relevance. At the same time, though, there are many well-filmed, well-acted and beautifully scored movies which appear to be culturally irrelevant (e.g., Kubrick's *Eyes Wide Shut* with Tom Cruise). So there was more than the fact that *Star Wars* was a "good film" behind its success.

But Lucas did pack his rather light, plot-thin film with relevant cultural themes: a solid grounding in what might be called the modern heroic tradition. The modern hero of *Star Wars* is, of course, Luke Skywalker. Seemingly of humble origins, he is a member of a "dysfunctional family" not unlike one might find in the average 20th-century home. He is secretly of privileged heritage, though, son of both a famous Jedi Knight and an heiress of a powerful dynasty. As he begins his quest to aid the mysterious Princess Leia, he gradually discovers his hidden gifts, and the good guys of the rebel alliance rapidly gather themselves around our hero. Even a "gray" character like Han Solo quickly resolves himself into an ally, if a bit self-centered. With the destruction of the Death Star a great wrong — the obliteration of Alderaan — has been righted, and justice prevails, if only to be challenged again by the re-emergence of Darth Vader.

Many critics have thoroughly documented that Lucas' story, slight as it is, borrows heavily from other sources; and Campbell himself noted that, rather than being startlingly original, *Star Wars* merely fits the prototypical model he wrote about in 1949. So what is it that made *Star Wars* so unique and powerful? It certainly isn't the modern heroic mode, which has been common enough in entertainment during the post-Vietnam years; and it certainly wasn't anything unique about the storyline itself. We may also safely say that it wasn't the characterizations or performances either, which clearly suffer when compared even to later offerings in the series.

Certainly one of the major factors was the ground-breaking and eye-popping technology. Even today, the original *Star Wars* effects hold up well with the contemporary counterparts. But there was also another significant factor attached to Lucas' technological genius, and that was his willingness to have the characters in his film hold their own technology at a respectable arm's length. The contrast between the Empire and the rebels is clear. Darth Vader and the Empire represent the logical and extreme ends of technological pursuits: the simultaneous ability to keep a body assembled and alive long after it has ceased to function properly on its own and the ability to fashion weapons of massive deadly force. Meanwhile, the rebellion mounts its resistance with technological tinkerers and goof-balls (think of Luke cleaning R2-D2, or Han Solo's less-than-dependable hyperspace drive in the "bucket of bolts" called "The Millennium Falcon"). The rebels are mostly motivated by a desire to simply go home.

Writer Regina Doman sees *Star Wars* expressing very nicely a cultural phenomenon which she calls the "Technological Death Wish."[35] Neither modernist in its embrace nor post-modernist in its rejection of technology, the "Technological Death Wish" lies in the ignored no-man's land between the two. It is best typified, perhaps, by the image of the imploding-exploding Death Star: a victory over the evils of technology, made possible only through the use of technology itself. The Rebel Alliance, it may be remembered, discovered the vulnerability of the Death Star through a computerized analysis of the space station's blueprints; and unlike the deadly microbes which destroy the alien invaders in H. G. Wells' *The War of the Worlds*, nature does not triumph over evil, technology itself does the job.

The "Technological Death Wish" expresses our culture's love-hate relationship with technology: the realization of the good which it has brought to modern life, but a loathing of the massive ills and destruction which it also brings.

But the truly unique aspect of *Star Wars*, as could empirically be determined by the constant repetition of the phrase on the lips of the movie's fans in 1977, was the novel expression, "May the Force be with you." The history of western philosophy has traditionally been seen as the struggle between Jerusalem and Athens, the tension between the rational and the metaphysical.[36] And while many scholars have seemed to accept, to a certain extent, Pascal's assertion that science and religion are two distinct domains of thought,[37] George Lucas presented the sage Obi Wan Kenobi embracing both mysticism and a light saber. At last: a religio-philosophical system that allowed our culture to have our cake, and eat it too! And what made the vision palatable even to agnostics and atheists was that the story was set not in our present or near future, but "long ago, in a galaxy far, far away."

So *Star Wars* is not a myth of who we are as a people, or who we will become, but a myth of where we came from, why we fear technology, and why we have an irrational thirst for spirituality. "I wanted to try to explain in a different way the religions that have already existed," Lucas has said. "I wanted to express it all."[38]

CONSECRATION ANALYSIS AND *STAR WARS*

So as a brief (and admittedly incomplete) case study, let us apply our proposed mode of analysis to *Star Wars;* and specifically, to "The Force." We will first address the biases which may influence our analysis; then we will address statements made by George Lucas regarding his intent, followed by a short analysis of The Force as presented in *Star*

Wars; and finally, we will draw conclusions as to how our analysis can point the way to God, either through affirmation or refutation.

We may, however, harbor biases affecting our objective assessment of The Force. The first may well be a certain ignorance of our faith's doctrine of the Holy Spirit; however, the various understandings of pneumatology will not here be addressed. A second, and almost as significant, bias may be a dogmatic tendency toward gut-response condemnation of doctrine which differs from our own. A third may be an apprehension of New Age spirituality; and a fourth may be a rather blind, post-modern thirst for the purely metaphysical. Depending on our biases, we may initially be either indifferent to, against, or attracted to Lucas' invention. Any of these predispositions will undoubtedly color our analysis of The Force, and should be kept at arm's length.

In turning to Lucas' intent, we must be cognizant both of his overall aims and his intent specifically in regard to The Force. Lucas, raised as a Lutheran, believes in God and pursues a personal faith; but he is hesitant to categorize himself as a Christian. With respect to The Force, Lucas has stated that his specific purpose was to use it to awaken people to metaphysical inquiry. As Lucas says, he "put the Force into the movie in order to try to awaken a certain kind of spirituality in young people — more a belief in God than a belief in any particular religious system." It was his desire "to make it so that young people would begin to ask questions about the mystery."[39] As far as Lucas understands God, then, and desires to be responsible to God, he is using his art to lead people in a similar direction. So, in Consecration Analysis, our first question asks: Is Lucas' intent specifically against God, or Christ? To the extent that we are able to extend mercy to those who may not understand God precisely in the way which we do, we may answer: Apparently not. And so, "whoever is not against us is for us."

Answering the second question of Consecration Analysis may often be a bit more difficult. Can Lucas, and his aims in creation of The Force, be said to be "with" Christ? Can we see in the person, life and acts of Christ anything which compares favorably with Lucas' use of The Force? A favorable comparison may be found in Jesus' words to Nicodemus in John 3, or His words to the woman at the well in John 4. Is there literal truth in Jesus' words that "you must be born again,"[40] or that the woman will "never thirst" again?[41] No, not any more than The Force, as Lucas intends it, is literally true. "I would hesitate to call the Force God," says Lucas. It's an avenue to exploration of "the larger mystery of the universe."[42]

This is not to say that Jesus' figurative words do not represent and lead to Truth: They certainly may, if one's heart is open to it. Nicodemus' heart was arguably less open to truth at this point in his life than it was later; and clearly less open to truth than the heart of the woman at the well, who enthusiastically exclaimed, "Give me this water."[43] In the same way, the viewer of *Star Wars* who is open to truth (in the metaphor of The Force) may respond: "I've never understood spirituality in that way; tell me more!" In Lucas' words, "you should be saying, 'I'm looking. I'm very curious about this, and I am going to continue to look until I can find an answer.'"[44] Nonetheless, the disinterested viewer may simply respond, "Whatever!" The effect is neither Lucas' fault, nor to his credit: it is in the heart of the audience.

Jesus Himself did not always begin with direct proclamation of the Kingdom of God. In many cases His aim was, through words and actions, to intrigue and then lead the responsive audience to the message of the kingdom, or the gospel. To the extent that Lucas' aim is to likewise intrigue his audience, it appears that he is "with" God, at the very least. And we find that Consecration Analysis produces a somewhat favorable result in the case of The Force. The analysis even provides us with some insight into how Jesus Himself, were He with us in body, might lead those intrigued by The Force into further truth.

Whether Lucas himself, in his films, ever moves on to "meatier" fare for those he has intrigued is beyond the scope of this short illustration, and it still remains for us to assess The Force for its limits as a useful spiritual metaphor. Just as physical birth and physical thirst are not in themselves perfect metaphors for a full understanding of the truth of Christ, neither is The Force. Probably the most direct and useful application of Lucas' metaphor is the spiritual reality that God truly is within all His people. To the unspiritual person, graphic demonstrations of the possibilities of being in touch with a "higher power" (such as Luke Skywalker's inspired destruction of the Death Star) might be an astounding revelation. Lucas, however, though thinking of The Force as a mythic element which may be "a more modern and easily accessible construct,"[45] never intended The Force as a correlate to the Holy Spirit. So there is no need for an elaborate demonstration of how The Force is inferior to the Christian doctrine of the Spirit. Instead, for the spiritually curious, The Force may simply serve as a departure point for further discussions of Christian faith; and, preferably, leading to elucidation of Whose spirit the Holy Spirit is, and how it becomes available to those who believe.

Having said that, it is probably useful to note that The Force owes as much of its origin to Eastern philosophy and religion, and the naturalistic dualism of (for example) the Yin and the Yang, as it does to Christian theology. "The issue of greed," Lucas says, "is the opposite of compassion — of not thinking of yourself all the time. These are the two sides — the good force and the bad force. They're the simplest parts of a complex cosmic construction."[46] Does this make The Force dangerous? Yes, in the same way that the knife on your kitchen counter is dangerous, or, at times, rather useful. It all depends on how one uses it, and perhaps on how one teaches others to handle it.

CONSECRATION ANALYSIS AND *THE LORD OF THE RINGS*

Application of Consecration Analysis to *The Lord of the Rings* will be both more complicated and more satisfying than this short examination of The Force. In particular, it will require not only a more thorough analysis of the text of Tolkien's substantial novel, it will also require a thorough understanding of the broader mythology behind the novel. The analysis is also complicated by the author's irascible, sometimes inconsistent published remarks with respect to the spirituality of his work, and perhaps by an unfamiliarity with Tolkien's own religious practice.

Yet the attempt should prove particularly rewarding, both to those who have embraced the power of the Ring without ever fully understanding why, and to those who have seen in Tolkien's work an intimidating, even insidious darkness. It may be surprising precisely where gold is found amidst the dross, and where other shiny bits prove nothing more than the sham of fool's gold.

To properly set the stage for our analysis, the next three chapters will be devoted to investigating popular biases in approaching Tolkien's work: that *The Lord of the Rings* is merely consummate storytelling; that Tolkien's work reflects an unapologetically anti-modern philosophy;

and that the average Christian understands Tolkien's own faith well enough to make snap judgments about Tolkien's aims. The chapter subsequent to these three will then proceed to the meat of Consecration Analysis for *The Lord of the Rings*, and will be followed by a chapter summarizing what may be the most disconcerting aspects of Tolkien's fiction. The book will then conclude with brief chapters summarizing alternate views, and the outcome of our analysis.

Chapter Two

A FANTASTIC MYTHOLOGY

Though they did not remain in contact during the later years of their lives, for a time J. R. R. Tolkien and celebrated Christian apologist C. S. Lewis were close and active friends. Together with writer Charles Williams, the three formed the core of a group called "The Inklings." Over a number of years, they met with other Christian academics on a fairly regular basis, in order to encourage one another and critique each other's work. For the would-be writers, publication of the works that would make each famous would be years away.

Decades later, and well after his conversion to Christianity, Lewis published an essay dissecting the value of Tolkien's fiction. Like Tolkien, Lewis appreciated myth. Its value, he said, "is that it takes all the things we know and restores to them the rich significance which has been hidden by 'the veil of familiarity.'"[1] Myth, then, is one of the means God provides to make his mercies new every morning, in much the same way that "the child enjoys his cold meat, otherwise dull to him, by pretending it is buffalo, just killed with his own bow and arrow."[2] Invention — and enjoyment — of myth can bring vitality to a faith that has long been quenched by the commonplace.

The invention process may not, however, be entirely pleasant. Certainly, Tolkien would have agreed with Joseph Campbell's assessment that "the very dreams that blister sleep boil up from the basic, magic ring of myth."[3] Tolkien many times described the birth of *The Lord of the Rings* as a purging, and was often at a loss to rationally account for much of its genesis. Hobbits, in particular, were an unlooked-for creation in Middle-Earth; the surprise which Treebeard expresses in his encounter with Merry and Pippin in Fangorn may well have mirrored Tolkien's own. "On a blank leaf I scrawled, 'in a hole in a ground there lived a hobbit,'" he famously recounted in a letter to W. H. Auden. "I did not and do not know why."[4]

This diminutive "branch of the specifically human race"[5] was particularly perplexing to Tolkien because of his preoccupation with what he described in 1916 as a "mad hobby": the development of "nonsense fairy language"[6] and the world in which this fairy language was used. It was well that this confession was made to the woman who would later be his wife, Edith Bratt, as she would necessarily become a long-suffering partner in the preparation and publishing of the author's celebrated works. A noted medieval philologist, Tolkien found outlet for his creative passions very early in life. There was likely never a time when his mind was not in some measure preoccupied with language, and his private "hobby" became responsible for his academic success. His obsession also spawned the vast back-story to *The Lord of the Rings*. "A real taste for fairy-stories was awakened by philology on the brink of manhood," Tolkien wrote, "and quickened to full life by war."[7] Tolkien's languages needed to be spoken by characters, and the characters needed to inhabit stories.

And so, "*The Hobbit* was not intended to have anything to do," said Tolkien, with "the 'mythology,' but naturally became attracted toward this dominant construction in my mind, causing the tale to become larger and more heroic as it proceeded."[8] Even after the unexpected success of the novel's publication, Tolkien would remark that "I don't much approve of *The Hobbit* myself, preferring my own mythology."[9]

To have developed a private, personal mythology may seem an extravagant claim on Tolkien's part; after all, we have seen that a key characteristic of the academic definition of "myth" is an ostensible basis in fact. *The Lord of the Rings* is fiction and is marketed as fantasy. Surely Tolkien was not so deluded as to confuse his "private and beloved nonsense" with "an elaborate and consistent mythology,"[10] was he? Well, yes. And no.

Tolkien's "basic passion" was for "myth (not allegory!) and for fairy-story, and above all for heroic legend on the brink of history."[11] This passion was dramatically expressed in a body of work unique in the history of English-language literature. So unique, in fact, as to lead us to consider with incredulity the reader who treats *The Lord of the Rings* as nothing more than a ripping good yarn.

FOUNDATIONAL ISSUES

In philosophy, one doesn't get far without understanding epistemology. A key aspect to this branch of philosophy is dealing with the "presuppositions and foundations" behind knowledge, to the extent that such presuppositions affect the validity of said knowledge. So it helps to understand, for example, when reading Nietzche, Marx, or Darwin, that the non-existence of the metaphysical, for them, is a given. These are men who believed they had reached definitive conclusions about the relation of the physical to the spiritual; and the spiritual simply didn't count. Their conclusions naturally follow, *if* one accepts their foundational premises. In the same way, the analysis which follows is based on two important issues.

First, *The Lord of the Rings* — grand in scope though it may be — is but a minute fragment of Tolkien's body of work. Aside from a handful of rather thin volumes, the vast majority of Tolkien's writing was related to Middle-Earth; and at present, this body of work now includes *The Hobbit*, *The Lord of the Rings*, *The Silmarillion*, *Unfinished Tales*, the twelve-volume *History of Middle-Earth*, and the oft-forgotten *Adventures of Tom Bombadil*. Further, the bulk of this work is of a different flavor from *The Lord of the Rings*, to even a greater extent than *The Hobbit* is a work of a different flavor than *The Lord of the Rings*. Why? Because the books were written for different audiences, and for different reasons.

While *The Hobbit* and *The Lord of the Rings* were deliberately prepared for publication (the former for children, and the latter for adults), the materials posthumously published in *The Silmarillion* and subsequent volumes were originally intended only for a very small and private audience: Tolkien himself and a small group of family and close associates. Consequently, the analysis which follows may seem outrageous to the reader familiar only with *The Lord of the Rings* and *The Hobbit*.

Second, we may be confident that Tolkien was a Christian. While a later chapter will be devoted to the specifics of Tolkien's beliefs, the analysis which follows presumes Tolkien's faith.

For those who don't consider Catholics Christians, I can only encourage consideration of the opinion of our Lord and Master, Jesus Christ: who does He consider with Him, and who does He consider against Him? If the prayers and sacrifices of Cornelius — a pagan — found favor with the Lord (and we know that Cornelius had an imperfect understanding of God), we may do well to be charitable in our treatment those who claim the name of Christ. Applying the apocalyptic epithet "the Whore of Babylon" to the Roman Catholic Church, and other such sectarian slander, is probably ill-advised in spite of historic precedent. The Accuser is often effective at clouding our human judgment with respect to this question.

TOLKIEN AND FANTASY

To begin with, let us examine the nature of Tolkien's fiction. What is the stuff of which it is made? J. R. R. Tolkien's Middle-Earth literature, *The Hobbit* and *The Lord of the Rings* in particular, are usually referred to and even marketed as fantasy. But would Tolkien himself think of his work only as fantasy? Traditionally, the genre has been defined as stories concerned with things which cannot, or could not, happen. This definition becomes problematic, though, as it would easily apply to the literature of classical mythology: the popular pejorative sense of the word "myth" has frequently been confused with "fantasy." After all, modern rationality tells us that much of the events described in Greek, Norse or even Judeo-Christian mythology could not have happened without the aid of supernatural forces which are "clearly" absent from the world as we know it.

Mythology, however, is not fantasy: the purpose of mythology is to provide a culture with an acceptable explanation for how that culture's world came to be. As we have seen, the creators of a mythology assert not only that the events described *could* happen, but ostensibly *did* happen.

It would be convenient, then, to simply levy upon fantastic literature the requirement that the story be concerned with a world other than our own, or that it take place only in the present or the future. But that would introduce unnecessary and equally problematic distinctions. Consider instead a definition of fantasy proposed by the author Joanna Russ: fantasy is a journey by a traveler (perhaps the reader) to a world so beautiful or wondrous that the traveler/reader wishes to — or does — stay in that fantastic world.[12] This definition excludes classical mythologies: they are not about an alternate reality, but about the past of the world that we know. Further, the "nuclear unit" of monomyth, by definition, includes separation, initiation *and return*.[13] Fantasy, then, is escapist, while mythology is reality-bound, if indirectly so. The distinction is useful, and appropriate.

This definition of fantasy, then, would appear to include *The Lord of the Rings*. But what about the author's opinion? As noted above, both *The Hobbit* and *The Lord of the Rings* are a very small part of Tolkien's life work; by his own account, they were "based on very elaborate and detailed workings, of geography, chronology and language."[14] Christopher Tolkien describes *The Silmarillion* and *Unfinished Tales* as "the central stories of the mythology" of Middle-Earth which "became long ago a fixed tradition, and background to later writings."[15] They represent "a completed and cohesive entity"[16] which suggests that the historical structure of Middle-Earth is an end in itself, and not the means to an end.[17] Christopher's opinions are well founded. In a commentary published for the first time in *Morgoth's Ring*, Volume X of *The History of Middle-Earth*, Tolkien himself stated that these "central stories" are "presented as 'histories,' or as accounts of what once was."[18] The best authorities we have on Tolkien, then, insist that the author viewed his work as mythology: an explanation for how the Middle-Earth of *The Lord of the Rings* came to be.

MYTH-MAKING AND MIDDLE-EARTH

As a philologist, Tolkien was also a noted translator of middle- and old-English works such as *Sir Gawain and the Green Knight* and *Sir Orfeo*. His study of the development of the English language led him to conceive his creation in the same vein: as middle-English has modulated into modern English, so also (Tolkien conceived) Middle-Earth has modulated into the modern world.

Upon first inspection, a person unfamiliar with middle-English may perceive similarities to modern English, but still might presume it a foreign language. In the same way, a person unfamiliar with the world of Middle-Earth can see similarities to our present world, but presumes it foreign to our own: a fantasy. This is precisely the effect that Tolkien intended; and just as the budding scholar is surprised to find the richness of connections between middle-English and modern English, the reader is pleasantly surprised, after the first flush of fantasy has passed, to find that the author purports Middle-Earth to be the earth of our own past.

Throughout his fiction, Tolkien identifies as the source of his story "The Red Book of Westmarch." The language Tolkien uses in describing this source is significant, as it occurs outside the scope of the text of the story:

> "This account of the Third Age is drawn mainly from the Red Book of Westmarch... so called because it was long preserved in the Undertowers, the home of the Fairbairns, Wardens of the Westmarch. It was in origin Bilbo's private diary, which he took with him to Rivendell. Frodo brought it back to the Shire, together with many loose leaves of notes, and during S.R. 1420-1 he nearly filled its pages with his account of the War. But annexed to it and preserved with it, probably in a single red case, were the three large volumes, bound in red leather, that Bilbo gave to him as a parting gift. ... The original Red Book has not been preserved, but many copies were made, especially of the first volume. ... The most important copy,

however... is an exact copy in all details of the Thain's Book in Minas Tirith. ... The Thain's book was thus the first copy made of the Red Book and contained much that was later omitted or lost."[19]

Following this passage is a lengthy and detailed history of the various copies of the Red Book, a kind of manuscript documentation that one finds in modern editions of the Bible. The veracity of the source documents is as important as the story itself, because the reliability of the manuscripts lends credence to the published text. A person equally ignorant of the Christian tradition and Tolkien's fiction would be hard-pressed to determine whether the Bible or *The Lord of the Rings* has better documented sources! This is remarkable, considering that Tolkien's sources do not exist.

Or do they? Tolkien is almost inscrutable in his consistency on this point. When Tolkien discusses the representation of the languages of Middle-Earth in an appendix to *The Return of the King*, he blithely explains that he has elected to "represent" the "Common Speech" with the use of modern English, the more archaic tongue of Rohan by old English, and so on.[20] He does not say he modeled Middle-Earth's languages on ours; he says he translated them based on corresponding relationships! Tolkien used the knowledge of his academic profession to create linguistic and literary connections between our world and that of Middle-Earth, so that the whole of his work could be viewed as "a compilation, a compendious narrative, made long afterwards from sources of great diversity (poems, and annals, and oral tales) that had survived in agelong tradition"[21] being passed down, finally, to himself. Tolkien scrupulously presents his history of Middle-Earth as an alternate mythology of our own world, not of some fantastic world.

Before proceeding, it is worthwhile to digress briefly to discuss the Historical Critical Method in more detail. One of the great theological projects of the 19th and 20th centuries has been the literary analysis of the source manuscripts of the Christian Bible. The development of the Historical Critical Method is a significant outgrowth of this effort. What the Method purports is that an analysis of various source manuscripts and their texts will yield a measure of their reliability. An offshoot of the Method is Source Criticism, which postulates theories about the actual sources of the stories found in the manuscripts that we do have. Source Criticism led in the 19th century to the postulation of a *Q manuscript*, a "true" history upon which the gospels were based. This Q manuscript, many academics claim, represents the only really reliable history of Jesus, and it is ostensibly lost to us forever. The Gospels of Matthew, Mark and Luke, according to the theory, are merely garbled versions of the "real" story.

I do not argue in favor of the Q theory. However, it is arguable that Tolkien's mythology represents, by way of analogy, what we may refer to as the *T-mythology*. Tolkien's work was not just intended to portray a convincing mythology of Middle-Earth; rather, it postulates a common source from which all the major Western mythologies could later be derived: Greek, Roman, Judeo-Christian, Norse, Finnish and Anglo-Saxon. Tolkien would not be likely to argue that he simply borrowed various elements from these mythologies and fused them into a comprehensive, cohesive unit; rather, as with his linguistic analysis of Middle-Earth, he would likely claim that the similarities are natural because the T-mythology predated, and represents the "truth" behind the others!

THE CORE ELEMENTS OF TOLKIEN'S MYTH

It would be easy at this point to conclude this analysis of Tolkien's mythology by merely observing that his work is still fiction, and that he knew it was fiction; and so the pretense which Tolkien maintains is just intended as great fun to help the reader willingly suspend disbelief. Or, perhaps, it would be convenient to observe that Tolkien's myth was intended, as mentioned previously, as legends "dedicated to England," and let things rest.

But understanding Tolkien's aim is key in understanding the cultural ramifications of his work, in appreciating the enormous impact his work has had. Is the willing suspension of disbelief his aim, or is it, perhaps, the not-so-willing suspension of other beliefs? And what place in the world did Tolkien see his native England occupying?

Consider the mythic fabric of the T-mythology.[22] Greek and Roman influences are dominant. The Valar are the equivalent of the gods of Olympus, being both male and female. Through direct intervention, they can control the earthly conditions, each being given his or her own realm of influence. The male gods are: Manwë, the god of the air, and senior in status, like Zeus; Ulmo, the Poseidon of the seas of Middle-Earth; Aulë, lord of the substances of the earth; Oromë, the hunter; Mandos, the keeper of the halls of the dead; Lórien, the god of dreams; and Tulkas, the wrestler and war god. The female gods are: Varda, goddess of light, and bride of Manwë; Yavanna, the goddess of fruit; Nienna, the keeper of sorrows; Estë, the healer; Vairë, the Weaver of stories; Vána, the goddess of youth; and Nessa, the Diana-like sister of Oromë. Though in Tolkien's conception they are created, "angelic beings," they are "as powerful as the 'gods' of human mythologies."[23]

While there is no one-to-one correspondence

between the Roman/Greek and T-mythology pantheons, the concept and organization is similar and hierarchical. There are greater orders of divinity, and lesser: the Maiar, who correspond to the nymphs, dryads and so on. The important similarity is that the gods of the T-mythology are, at the beginning, intimately connected to the world and directly influence the course of its events, even directing battles much as the gods do in Homer.

Tolkien borrows from Norse mythology as well. Aulë is essentially Thorian in character: the god of the forge and the wielder of the hammer. It is he who creates the Dwarves, as one would expect since Dwarves are central to Norse mythology. Tolkien draws the very names of the Dwarves, and other characters, straight from Norse legends: Durin, Thráin, Thror, Fili, Kili, Bifur, Bofur, Dáin, even Gandalf.[24]

Naturally, though, the most noticeable influence on the T-mythology is Anglo-Saxon. The codes of behavior, modes of dress and of battle, and style of architecture draw heavily from both historical and fictional accounts of that period: hosts of knights in shining armor, fire-breathing dragons in the tradition of Beowulf, and the Faerie land of Aman. The two most dominant aspects of the T-mythology are Anglo-Saxon: the Elves themselves, and the concept of the paradisical west. In Arthurian legend, the dead king himself sails into the west and is never seen again; and in Middle-Earth, the land of the gods is in the west: even most Elves hail in ancestry to the blessed land of Aman.

So to what extent does Christian mythology inform the T-mythology? Very troublingly, Tolkien, in connection with his desire to construct English legends, stated that Arthurian legend is imperfect because "it is involved in, and explicitly contains the Christian religion."[25] Christian elements are not entirely missing, however.

Much has historically been made of Tolkien's association with C. S. Lewis, and the hand which Tolkien had in bringing the former agnostic to Christ. A popular but misguided presumption is that Lewis' overt, intense Christian spirituality somehow rubbed off on Tolkien, and similarly found its way into his work. Just as Narnia's Aslan is an allegory for Christ (so the theory goes), Tolkien also "veiled" the Christianity of his mythology in allegory. Aside from the fact that Tolkien's aims were different from Lewis' aims, and that Tolkien's own passion was for "myth (not allegory!)," such a claim is not supported by the evidence.

Yes, there is extensive Christian symbolism both in the text of *The Lord of the Rings* and throughout the T-mythology. Thematic influences abound, but the only structural vestiges of the Judeo-Christian tradition in the T-mythology are: first, a monotheistic conception of one supreme, all-powerful god, Eru-Ilúvatar, who is above the Ainur and not embodied; second, a class of angelic beings, the Ainur; and third, the evil one in the world, Melkor, a former vassal ("fallen angel") who challenges Eru, corrupts many of the Maiar, and is forever cast from paradise. However, these influences are more purely Hebraic than uniquely Christian: aside from a vague prophetic text or two (discussed more fully later), Eru never condescends to walk the earth in the form of a man and sacrifice himself for man's salvation (the core story of the gospel, Christian myth); and Melkor is chained and cast into the void long before the time of Frodo's Middle-Earth, rather than as the culminating work of the incarnate Lord. Most notably, perhaps, Eru is neither mentioned nor implied within the text of *The Lord of the Rings!*

It may be argued that Gandalf is a Christ-figure; but Gandalf is not Eru incarnate. He is instead one of the Maiar, simply in the appearance of an old man; and it is not Gandalf who saves mankind, but the Hobbit, Frodo. When Gandalf leaves, he offers no spiritual assistance to men. By the Third Age and the time of the War of the Ring, Eru does not figure in the speech of any race; and the only overt religious practice of men is a moment of silence facing west at mealtimes (a practice which, aside from the direction faced, recalls Islam more than Christianity). Whatever similarities the T-mythology has to the Judeo-Christian tradition are only a means to an end, and are no more significant than obvious parallels to other mythologies.

For Tolkien, this is a necessity: England is older than Christianity; therefore, meaningful legends for England must be pre-Christian. While they may be compatible with proto-Judeo myth, and may even point forward to Christ in much the same way that the Old Testament does, Tolkien's stories cannot encompass the Christian myth.

AN ASTONISHING GOAL

And this is the whole point: if one enters "Secondary Belief" and accepts Tolkien's contention that the T-mythology is, in fact, an actual mythology of earth, two conclusions present themselves. First, it is conceivable that the whole of Western mythology (Greco-Roman, Norse, Anglo-Saxon, Judeo-Christian, etc.) could have been literary descendants from the T-mythology. The T-mythology not only explains how the Middle-Earth of *The Lord of the Rings* came to be, but also posits a common source for the mythologies which other cultures developed to explain the conditions of their worlds. From a strictly literary standpoint, this is an astonishing goal magnificently and fantastically realized.

But this conclusion does not account for Tolkien's stated purpose. Tolkien's myth for England was not for a people long dead; his myth was intended to provide meaning for 20th-century England. In conceiving the T-mythology, Tolkien must have seen a need to create a new mythology for the modern world. He perceived that the existing western mythologies, including the Judeo-Christian tradition, failed to account for the England that he knew. Tolkien was not satisfied with merely explaining how things got to be at the time of the War of the Ring.

Consider that the period of the War of the Ring presents Middle-Earth in a time of transition. Physically, the structure of earth is far from settled.

> "Those days, the Third Age of Middle-Earth, are now long past, and the shape of all lands has been changed; but the regions in which the Hobbits then lived were doubtless the same as those in which they still linger: the North-West of the Old World, east of the Sea."[26]

More significant, however, is the fact that Middle-Earth is undergoing drastic *metaphysical* changes: magic exists, yes; but it is fading fast. The T-mythology, then, serves not only to explain how coercive supernatural forces, both good and evil, came into and shaped our world; it is the tale of how people came to believe that these magical forces *have left our world.*

"In the beginning," so to speak, Eru created Middle-Earth, and the Valar were sent to shape it, to care for its people, and to battle Melkor-Morgoth and his evil forces. The Valar were in the world and intimately related to all its workings. By the time of the War of the Ring, however, the Valar had defeated Melkor, withdrawn from Middle-Earth, and removed their blessed land of Aman from contact with earth. They sent as emissaries the Maiar Istari, the wizards, to finally defeat the last followers of the defeated Melkor. The only divine presences in the world are the wizards, Tom Bombadil, balrogs, and Sauron himself.

The Elves, though in essence immortal, are not divine. They can die if wounded mortally enough, or if they lose the will to live. For the Elves in Middle-Earth, immortality is in fact a curse. They know that their time is drawing to a close, and that they will soon have to leave their chosen homes, returning to the land of their ancestors, Aman; for some, such as Elrond, Celeborn and Galadriel, this means having to leave a place they have called home for more than 3,000 years. Though they love Middle-Earth, they know that it is not theirs, that ultimately it belongs to men. The full significance of the tragedy is played out twice in the T-mythology: first, in the prophetic tale of Beren and Lúthien; and second, in the fulfilled prophecy of Arwen and Aragorn. Though long-lived, Aragorn is still mortal. When he dies, his Elvish bride Arwen loses her will to live, and sacrifices her immortality.[27]

The episode at the Grey Havens at the conclusion of *The Return of the King* foreshadows the full vision of the T-mythology. As Gandalf says to Aragorn,

> "Though much has been saved, much must now pass away; and the power of the Three Rings also is ended. And all of the lands that you see, and those that lie round about them, shall be the dwellings of Men. For the time comes for the Dominion of Men, and the [Elves] shall fade or depart. ... The Third Age was my age. I was the Enemy of Sauron; and my work is finished. I shall go soon. The burden must lie now upon you and your kindred."[28]

Following the War of the Ring, almost all of the

Elves do leave, and with them (and the power of the Three Rings) disappear the paradisical Lothlórien and Rivendell; the Ents are doomed to extinction; and eventually, even the Hobbits disappear, avoiding men "with dismay and... becoming harder to find."[29] The Scouring of the Shire prefigures modern social action: it is collective resistance against tyranny which cures the Hobbits' ills, and magic at best only helps the healing. When Sam Gamgee returns home for the final time, it is with a certain poignancy; for the world that he returns to is no longer the world that he knew. The Fourth Age will be far more mundane than the supernaturally-driven Third Age.

The agents of evil have been destroyed, of course; but at the same time, active, intercessive good has been banished as well. The supernatural has all but gone. Small traces still exist, but even those are fated to eventually degenerate so as to become all but indiscernible. Is there hope for the future? Perhaps, but it is vague at best, and never discussed openly. The future of Middle-Earth lies in our secular present: a world in which there is little or no evidence of the great supernatural forces which our myths tell us once shaped the earth. As Robert Foster puts it, Tolkien documents "the progressive freeing of Man from the influence of both Valar and demons to work out his own destiny."[30] By design, the T-mythology explains an increasingly mechanized, sadly secular England.

Tolkien was not at all enthused about the industrialization of rural England; and he could clearly see that his nation was not Christian. The Christianity of the T-mythology, then, is largely symbolic. It is more ethical than spiritual. The T-mythology presents, in fact, a pre-Christian world which is remarkably similar to the post-Christian world: one free to postulate God's removal from the world; one free to champion men as the only agents of evil, or good; one free to deny the miraculous, and emasculate the Holy Spirit. Where is forgiveness? Where is prayer? Where is ritual worship? Tolkien bemoans a purely rational age in which man believes he is simply left to master himself.

NOT JUST A STORY

At the same time, many find Tolkien's work a hopeful encouragement: an expression of a deep yearning for our more spiritual past. Tolkien understands that the spiritual past of our modern secular world does not lie primarily in Christian models, but in a more universal (if purely western) embrace. He knew that contemporary thought, even much religious practice, is naturally shackled in such a way that it can only pay lip service to the supernatural. Tolkien did not endorse what he saw around him, of course; his eyes were wide open, and what he saw troubled him.

The astounding popular reaction to Tolkien's work, now moving into the 21st century, may in fact be part of a post-modern response to the extreme rational bent of modernism. Tolkien's readers, like the author himself, have not personally embraced a vision of a spiritually impoverished present. Rather, his readers seemingly embrace the hope of recapturing a spirituality which truly believes that all things are possible: that our possibilities are not bounded by what scientists (or our parents) tell us can or can't happen.

Tolkien is to be taken at his word that he wanted to develop a meaningful mythology for England, and to be taken seriously. The design of his fiction has been proven to be mightily effective and far more important and potent in both scope and impact than any mere adventure story. Tolkien's Hobbits serve as a cultural bridge from Middle-Earth into the modern era. His myth simultaneously accounts for what our culture has lost, and what it still may regain.

The foundation of modernism is the Cartesian proposition that knowledge, not truth, will set us free: "I think, therefore I am." For Tolkien, this was not enough. "I believe that legends and myths are largely made of 'truth,'" he asserted, "and indeed present aspects of it that can only be received in this manner."[31]   If anything, Tolkien's mythology was a grand project conceived in response to the more destructive effects of modernism, as we shall presently see in more detail.

Tolkien's body of work represents perhaps the most inventive fiction written since moveable type was introduced. Claiming that he was "simply being creative" in producing it would be akin to stating that ceiling of the Sistine Chapel is "just a painting." We may be justifiably intrigued by the workings of an artist's mind consumed by such a vision.

Chapter Three

TOLKIEN AND MODERNITY

In Aeschylus' classic Greek drama, *Prometheus Bound*, Oceanus tells the distraught hero, "Words are the physicians of a mind diseased" — or something to that effect. It is remarkable that a line written so many thousands of years ago could so eloquently express the dynamic tension between creative impulse and rationality. Whose mind, after all, was diseased? That of Prometheus?

What about Oceanus? How could he know of such disease if his own mind were not diseased? Perhaps the truly diseased mind was that of Aeschylus. Or perhaps the disease is in the words themselves, a notion popularly expressed in the title of Laurie Anderson's song, "Language is a Virus."[1]

After all, Oceanus' words can be variously translated as "words are the physicians of a mind diseased," or "words are the physician of a wrath-sick soul" — even, most literally, "of wrath's disease wise words the healers are."[2] Which of these translations comes closest to expressing Aeschylus' mind, and how does a translation reflect the mind of the translator? And how can a writer anticipate the mind of the reader, and the inevitable warping of the words that take place in that similarly "diseased" quarter?

Certainly, if we can gauge the significance of a creative work by the impact it has had within the culture, we must admit that the things which Tolkien wrote, and the things which he said about what he wrote, raise some of the most thought-provoking issues in 20th-century literature and religion. It would be well, then, to understand the nature of the specific disease — one of society, as well as the mind — which Tolkien's words were intended to assuage: the disease of modernity.

THE MODERN PERIOD DEFINED

In the most general sense, the modern period is understood to be the epoch birthed by the philosophical writings of René Descartes. Often equated in the vernacular with "The Enlightenment," this epoch is also described as "The Age of Reason." Principally, its genesis was the West's emergence from the Dark Ages, and the natural opportunity which prosperity allowed for the pursuit of activities not directly related to survival. One such activity was the luxury of thinking, purely for the sake of thinking; and during the Renaissance, much of the great thinking of the Classical period was rediscovered: Plato, Aristotle, Augustine.

The cultural shift that this re-awakening represented might be best understood in the frustration of a child who lives with an irrational parent. "Do as you are told!" does not satisfy the instinctive need to understand and be understood, and being punished for behavior which is encouraged or ignored in others is confusing. Reasonable answers to the endless "whys" always come as a breath of fresh air, even if the new regime does not yield an ideal environment.

The Cartesian license to think was a much needed breath of fresh air. Gone was the centuries-long enforced tyranny over the mind. Suddenly, men were free (if only men, and only some of them) to question the seemingly arbitrary rules of feudal and episcopal systems. They were free to propose new systems of thought for the governance of mind and society. Within a very short time, differing schools of thought proliferated. While all the great thinkers agreed that thinking about thinking was good, and that increased knowledge would benefit mankind, there was widely divergent thought about the very nature of knowledge. So, while modernism asserts that the human mind can know truth, inherent in modernism is the insistence on diversity of thought: the seeds of relativism. To suggest that truth is definitive and bounded would represent a return to the Dark Ages. Of course, freedom of thought is something of a Pandora's box, as seen in the language of philosophy.

For example, the branch of modern thought known as *materialism* is popularly understood as an affinity for things, the need to accumulate stuff. So in light of starving children in "third world" countries, the word "materialism" now often carries a negative connotation. Materialism has at its foundations, however, Hobbes' rather more disturbing notion that *the spiritual does not exist*: only the material world that our senses perceive is real. Such a philosophy, when pursued to its extreme, has no room for the spiritual question, "What good is it for a man to gain the whole world, yet forfeit his soul?"[3] This metaphysical dismissal is not quite the same thing as occasional indulgence in unnecessary extravagance. But such is one facet of modernism.

Similarly, we tend to think of *empiricism* merely as the means by which scientific data are gathered: experiments are designed, and the results are empirically observed and recorded as the basis for evaluation of an hypothesis. And this is good. It allows scientific progress. Yet modern scientific method grew out of a school of thought championed at various times, and in various forms, by John Locke and John Stuart Mill (among others): formal empiricism. Mill's basic premise was that *the foundation of all knowledge was the perception of the senses.* Pure empiricism rejects all purported knowledge having, as its basis, a source other than our own faculties. The Apostle

Paul, then, would be mistaken to assert that we "see but a poor reflection as in a mirror."[4] The empiricist would claim that what we see — what our eyes perceive — is the reality itself. It is not some imperfect glimpse of metaphysical, spiritual reality. And such is another facet of modernity.

Even the supposed bogey-man of *existentialism* — the philosophical assertion that the individual is the only proper arbiter of knowledge, truth and existence — is an outgrowth of modern thought; and while we may recoil at such an extreme philosophy, we can find no refuge in other modern philosophies, such as *pragmatism* or *idealism*. The former asserts that the outcome of an action is the sole measure of its value; but such outcome may be perceived differently depending, for instance, on whether you are a Jew or a Nazi. By contrast, idealism tells us, in its most radical form, that the physical world is merely a perception of mental reality; and so it is no surprise (and no great wrong) that one person's pleasure can simultaneously result in another person's pain. If it feels good, do it!

Such a brief treatment of modernism is, of course, overly facile and wildly incomplete. But it is sufficient to demonstrate that day-to-day living tends to hinder philosophical reflection. The implications are sobering, because "professional" thinkers are left to architect major cultural shifts, and the systems of thought they propose perpetuate the intellectual hierarchy. Catch-22.

We benefit from philosophical progress, and we suffer from it as well. Modern thought has simultaneously allowed the development of vaccines, yet led to anxiety about anthrax in our mail; it has allowed us to design earthquake-resistant buildings, yet not prevented the collapse of the twin towers of the World Trade Center; and it has made possible both the United Nations and the ever-present threat of global thermonuclear war. Progress, yes, but at what cost?

THE POST-MODERN RESPONSE

The modern period, of course, has not been charac-terized by wholesale, consistent embrace of its tenets. Since Descartes, in fact, a number of influential movements against the press of modernity have been popular. In phi-losophy and art, perhaps the earliest and most pervasive was *romanticism*: a belief that *truth may be found in all nature*, and perhaps least of all in the mind of man. Romantics endorsed emotion and imagination, waxed nostalgic for the past, embraced the mysterious. Socially, the most virulent reactionaries were the Luddites, who literally waged war against Victorian industrialists. Many British factories were burned because common people revolted against the effects of mechanized progress.

So in reality, post-modernism represents a continuity of thought, not some radically new philosophical develop-ment. What distinguishes post-modernism from its prede-cessors is merely an openly articulated acknowledgment and rejection of modernism. This overt rejection was not possible for the romantics, because modern thought was still in the process of being formulated, and was not yet recog-nized as an "-ism." It was also not possible for the Luddites, because they were rebelling against mechanical symptoms not schools of thought. Post-modernism, however, specifi-cally rejects "the Enlightenment's confidence in the achievement of objective human knowledge through reliance upon reason."[5] Why?

The origins of post-modernism may be compared to a young family. They build a house in a new neighborhood, thinking they've finally found their dream home. Everything about the place is wonderful; however, the first spring they are there, they notice that the neighbors' yards aren't particularly well kept. They are infested with dande-lions. Their own lawn is all right; the dandelions are just in the neighbors' lawns, so at first they are a bit disappointed but still confident that this is the right neighborhood for them. The next spring, however, they are dismayed to discover that the noxious weeds have spread to their own lawn. What's worse, the dandelions aren't the tiny yellow flowers they noticed in the neighbor's yard; they have now become the size of small trees. Every aspect of their lives becomes dominated by the dandelions, and the ever-present threat to peace they represent. Several of the family's children die in accidents, trying to combat the dandelions. Worse, the family discovers that the giant dandelions aren't really an invasive weed; they're an indigenous species. They go with the neighborhood. The remaining children discover that their parents' reluctance to move (and admit they are wrong) is responsible for their continuing misery. They are convinced they must move to a new neighborhood; and while they don't know precisely what kind of a neighborhood they're looking for, they just know it won't be like the one their folks chose.

So what were the first signs of the dangers of modernism? The evils of the industrial revolution were ominous warnings; but the most serious symptoms — the "giant dandelions" of modernism, if you will — became obvious in the mechanized, chemical campaigns of World War I, and they flourished during the inhumanity of the Depression. As American novelist Booth Tarkington described it,

> "In New York a stockbroker leaped from a window as high above the ground as had flown the wares in which he dealt. The wares did worse than fall; being made of airy vapors, they dispersed themselves — and other brokers jumped. These things were not the causes of the historic long Depression that was to last ten years; they were only surface symptoms."[6]

With the genocide of World War II and the advent of the nuclear age, the killer dandelions of modernism were unavoidable, and humanity had only itself to blame. The so-called "Enlightenment Project" was declared a failure, and new philosophical neighborhoods were needed.

Interestingly, post-modernism doesn't suggest any new answers; it just rejects some of the old ones. "The significant problems that we face," Einstein allegedly observed, "cannot be solved by the same level of thinking which created them." And so post-modernism concludes that systems of thought founded purely on a trust of human reason are automatically excluded from consideration. Perhaps systematic thought itself must be excluded.

MODERNISM IN LITERATURE

It might be tempting to interpret Tolkien's literary critique of modernism as either reactionary or visionary. In the former case, it would be easy to dismiss the critique as neo-romanticism, and in the latter we might interpret Tolkien as pre-post-modern. To put Tolkien in the proper context, however, we must consider the age in which Tolkien was writing. Were the concerns which he expressed commonly held, or was he a voice crying in the wilderness?

Consider the typical dinner-time conversation. Today, a family might discuss the "war on terrorism," the high salaries of professional athletes, or the latest murder / kidnapping. If the family is having trouble with its adolescent children, the conversation may turn to music and movies, and thereby to the apparent lack of respect that kids have for anything. It might also turn to the near-epidemic of high-school dropouts. Don't these kids think of their future? Do they think they can flip hamburgers the rest of their lives? Don't they have any ambition? And if the family is politically or philosophically oriented, the conversation could then turn to cultural and moral relativism, Generation X, and the supposedly chilling effects of post-modernism.

America and Modernism

Eighty years ago, similar conversations were also taking place around American dinner tables. The flavor, however, was likely to be different. An example can be found in the writing of Booth Tarkington. Once considered the "Dean of American Letters," the novelist was famous for capturing the people of middle America and their sentiments in Pulitzer-prize-winning fashion. His novels *The Magnificent Ambersons* and *Alice Adams*, among many others, were later made into legendary and Oscar-winning movies. Courtesy of Mr. Tarkington, let's eavesdrop into a conversation of the Eliot family, somewhere in Indiana, around 1916. Mrs. Eliot is trying to persuade her daughter Muriel of the merits (and eligibility) of a young man across the street.

"Your father and I do wish you could feel more kindly toward the poor boy, Muriel."

"Well, I can't, and I don't want to. What's more, I wouldn't marry him if I did."

"Not if you were in love?"

"Poor mamma!" Muriel said compassionately. "What has love to do with marrying? I expect to retain my freedom; I don't propose to enter upon a period of child-rearing —"

"Oh, good gracious!" Mrs. Eliot cried. "What a way to talk!"

"But if I did," Muriel continued, with some sharpness, "I should never select Renfrew Mears to be my assistant in the task. And as for what you call 'love,' it seems to me a rather unhealthy form of excitement that I'm not subject to, fortunately."

"You *are* so queer," her mother murmured; whereupon Muriel laughed.

No doubt her laughter was a little condescending. "Queer?" she said. "No — only modern. Only frank and wholesome! Thinking people look at life as it really is, nowadays, mamma. I am a child of the new age; but more than that, I am not the slave of my emotions; I am the product of my thinking. Unwholesome excitement and queer fancies have no part in my life, mamma."

"I hope not," her mother responded with a little spirit. "I'm not exactly urging anything unwholesome upon you, Muriel. You're very inconsistent, it seems to me."

"I!" Muriel said haughtily. ... "The one thing I *won't* be called," she said, "is 'inconsistent!'"

"Well, but —"

"I won't!" she cried, and choked. "You *know* it makes me furious; that's why you do it!"

"Did I understand you to say you never permitted your emotions to control you?" her mother asked dryly.[7]

Not every young person in 1916 was like Muriel, of course; thank God! But if Tarkington's portrayal of the girl could be easily perceived as humorous by the readers of *Red Book* or *McCall's*, the caricature was common enough. As the World War I generation was maturing into young adulthood, modernism was as much of a concern to their parents as post-modernism is to parents today.

Common Concerns About Modernism

The aspect of modernism that most absorbed Tarkington's thinking, though, was not its effect upon youth, but its effect upon the landscape of his native middle America, much as Tolkien was concerned about its effect on his English countryside. For Tarkington, the symbol of modernism was smoke.

> "There is a midland city in the heart of fair, open country, a dirty and wonderful city nesting dingily in the fog of its own smoke. The stranger must feel the dirt before he feels the wonder, for the dirt will be upon him instantly. It will be upon him and within him, since he must breathe it, and he may care for no further proof that wealth is here better loved than cleanliness; but whether he cares or not, the negligently tended streets incessantly press home the point, and so do the flecked and grimy citizens. At a breeze he must smother in whirlpools of dust, and if he should decline at any time to inhale the smoke he has the meagre alternative of suicide."[8]

The smoke of Tarkington's 1922 midland came, of course, from the burgeoning factories. As smoke was a tangible, terrible symbol for modern progress, it was also symptomatic of the pursuit of wealth. What does it profit a man to gain the world, and begrime the neighborhood in which he lives?

Naturally, things were not so different on the East side of the Atlantic. One of the more enigmatic characters in *The Lord of the Rings* is Tom Bombadil. Understanding the role of Bombadil within Tolkien's fiction is one of the keys to unlocking Tolkien's similar objection to technology: the inevitable environmental damage attendant to such "progress." In a letter to Stanley Unwin, the publisher of

The Hobbit, Tolkien said that Bombadil represented "the spirit of the (vanishing) Oxford and Berkshire countryside."[9] Tolkien portrays this proto-industrialized countryside in the state of the Shire upon Frodo's return, with the other Hobbits, following the War of the Ring. Ominously, it is the poison of Saruman's words which has indirectly ravaged the Hobbits' Eden. Of course, the offenders must be cast out, and paradise must be regained under the supervision of Samwise Gamgee, the Great Gardener. We would be incorrect, however to conclude that Tolkien's technological aversion was symptomatic of a general anti-modernist, even incipient post-modernist, bent.

TOLKIEN'S RESPONSE TO MODERNISM

Tolkien, like so many of the young men of his generation, saw more than enough inhumanity in the trenches of France. It was during this period, as we have observed earlier, that Tolkien's mythology was "quickened to full life" from the seeds of his tragic childhood. "There are other things more grim and terrible to fly from," he wrote, "than the noise, stench, ruthlessness, and extravagance of the internal-combustion engine. There are hunger, thirst, poverty, pain, sorrow, injustice, death."[10] Tolkien found both war and industrial blight tangibly evil.

To what did Tolkien turn in order to help make sense of the nightmarish struggle? Consider Tarkington's Muriel Eliot, circa 1916: "Her mind spent the greater part of its time in half-definite dreaming, and although she did not suspect such a thing, her romantic imagination was the abode in which she really dwelt," Tarkington wrote. "What she really wanted was a fairy story."[11] And so did Tolkien in 1917. "I took to 'escapism,'" he said, "or really transforming experience into another form and symbol with Morgoth and Orcs and the Eldalie."[12] Long before he had formulated the rigorous theory expressed in his essay "On

Fairy Stories," Tolkien was using the familiar romantic literary form as therapy during his weeks in the military hospital.

The history in which Europe, England, and Tolkien were steeped is indeed a darker sort than that which Americans can perhaps wholly grasp. While we watch, in rapt fascination, Ken Burns' remastered epic Civil War documentary on the Public Broadcasting Service, and are perhaps incapacitated by the loss of life inflicted on 9/11, European historians are likely to remain unmoved. At Verdun alone more than 100,000 bodies *could not be identified*. So when Tolkien said, "I love England (not Great Britain and certainly not the British Commonwealth),"[13] he was expressing his love for the British countryside and the values of its common folk; but he was excluding the historic colonialism, imperialism and nationalism behind almost 2000 continuous years of European carnage. The Age of Reason, in particular, promised to put an end to such atrocities. It didn't.

It's natural that Tolkien should turn in self-defense to literary romanticism, in which dreams and desires prevail over everyday realities. While Tolkien was recovering from "trench fever," they did. And more than one critic has noted the force of "Tolkien's Christianized romantic imagination"[14] in shaping his work. Robert J. Reilly was not alone in arguing, in fact, that *The Lord of the Rings* "is at least partly an attempt to restore the hero to modern fiction."[15] Oddly enough, Reilly sees Tolkien's work as a major *contribution* to modern literature, not a reaction *against* modernity. How could Tolkien's work possibly be understood as a modern fiction? Because, as his own son has pointed out, Tolkien "was devising — from within it — a fearful weapon against his own creation."[16]

TOLKIEN AS A POST-MODERN WRITER

Critical attempts to cast Tolkien as a modern writer, however may be severely misguided. "It is dangerous for an individual to assume that any attempted work of art," Booth Tarkington observed, "actually is what it appears to himself. I have known a child to assume that his grandfather, kneeling for prayers, was a horse to be mounted and ridden."[17] At the same time, such is precisely the domain of literary criticism. Reilly is justified in pointing out that the "aim of the critic, as [G. K.] Chesterton once remarked, is to show what the artist did, whether the artist meant to do it or not."[18]

Roger Sale, one of the sages under whom I studied at the University of Washington, went so far as to claim, "In any study of modern heroism, if J. R. R. Tolkien's *The Lord of the Rings* did not exist it would have to be invented."[19] Why? Precisely because of the stultifying effects of modernism. Despite the historic importance of our cultural myths, Joseph Campbell says, in the modern age "these mysteries have lost their force; their symbols no longer interest our psyche. The notion of a cosmic law, which all existence serves and to which man himself must bend," he continues, has been supplanted by models of thought expressed purely "in mechanical terms."[20] In other words, the Cartesian model of the universe has won out over the unwieldy power of myth, which is not "reasonable."

Campbell does not argue, however, that we have abandoned the need for myth in the modern age. Instead, he insists that our persistent need for myth has led us to reformulate its basic constructs in ways which are more palatable to a modern sensibility. While the primary purpose of Mosaic myth, for instance, was to provide meaning for the individual Israelite within the context of country and religion, modern myth becomes about the need of the individual to reshape and restore meaning to his culture. "It is not society that is to guide and save the creative hero, but precisely the reverse,"[21] Campbell argues.

In his analysis of *The Lord of the Rings*, Sale puts it a bit more cryptically: "We see, without in the least needing to make the seeing into a formulation, what the heroism of our time is and can be: lonely, lost, scared, loving, willing, and compassionate — to bind oneself to the otherness of others by recognizing our common livingness."[22]

It is telling, perhaps, that many of the advocates of a modernist reading of Tolkien (Sale in particular) focus on Frodo Baggins as the hero of the story. This is probably natural, as it is appealing to identify with a "hero" who has very good intentions; but who also, at the precise moment when character is most needed, is unable to rise to the occasion. Frodo himself does not cast the Ring into the flames of Orodruin. It is Providence, in the form of Gollum, after all, that saves the day; or perhaps Mercy, in the restraint which has earlier prevented both Bilbo and Frodo from taking the creature's life. Frodo is like us, but he still saves the day.

Nonetheless, Frodo is not the hero of Tolkien's story, appealing as the traits of his character and struggle may be. The hero of the story, for Tolkien, is Samwise Gamgee. Hobbits are, after all, a distillation of "comicness, peasantry, and if you will… Englishry," and Sam is a "jewel among the Hobbits."[23] So Tolkien is abundantly clear in his mind that "the simple 'rustic' love of Sam and his Rosie (nowhere elaborated) is absolutely essential to the study of his (the chief hero's) character, and to the theme of the relation of ordinary life (breathing, eating, working, begetting) and quests, sacrifice, causes, and the 'longing for elves' and sheer beauty."[24]

This important observation, however, does not

entirely negate the conclusions of Sale and company (though it certainly discredits a great deal of how they got from point A to point B). Bilbo and Frodo are not modern heroes at all. They are both classic exponents of the "nuclear unit" of Campbell's pre-modern monomyth, demonstrating through their adventures the same heroic pattern of separation, initiation and return demonstrated by Homer's Ulysses. But there is no initiation with Sam. While his separation from the Shire does satisfy many of his basic longings (for Elves, and for beauty), Sam is not transformed by his experience. Unlike Bilbo, he is not fully initiated into the ways of the folk living east of the Shire. And unlike Frodo, Sam is entirely content, upon his return to Hobbiton, to settle into the "ordinary life" of breathing, eating, working and begetting. One can imagine Sam holding court at the Golden Dragon in his later years as mayor, saying, "The War of the Ring was an awesome and fateful thing, I'll not deny. It was a great thing that Frodo done, it was. And you, too, Mister Merry. And Mister Pippin, begging your pardon. But if we hadn't come home to my Rosie, and my garden, and the Gaffer, why, I'm not sure what it all would have been about."

So Campbell's theory is sadly correct: the larger society does not guide and save Sam Gamgee at all; in fact, if it weren't for the more conventionally heroic bent of Gandalf, Aragorn and even Frodo, Sam wouldn't have been involved in such affairs himself. Even after it is all over, and in spite of the role that Sam played in the struggle, Sam would just as soon society left him alone. Everyday life is enough for him. He has no desire to dwell in Imladris, nor incapacitating wounds which drive him to sail into the west (though he does so, later, after living a long and full life). He has no vision for a radically new Shire, but works to restore it to what it was before the war. And Campbell is right: this is a new kind of heroism, in which the consistency of the individual saves society. Sam is not a hero because he is transformed into something else; he is a hero because he *isn't* transformed. Sam is affected, of course; but he is still Sam Gamgee, a gardener.

Sam is Tolkien's hero, then, because Sam is Tolkien. If it weren't for the more conventionally heroic bent of English, French and German wags and politicians, Tolkien would never have been involved in such affairs as World War I. And when it was all over, and in spite of the arguably heroic role that Tolkien himself played in the war, he would just as soon society left him alone, and progressed without him. Everyday life is enough for Tolkien. "I do not really belong inside my invented history," he said; and were he to be offered the chance, he would reply, "I do not wish to!"[25]

It is doubtful, of course, that Tolkien himself would have seen Sam as the culmination of heroic development in modern literature, particularly since Campbell's groundbreaking work was not published until *The Lord of the Rings* was largely completed. Nonetheless, Tolkien's own modernist bent would come into play following the astonishing success of the publication of *The Lord of the Rings*.

TOLKIEN AS A MODERN RATIONALIST

Tolkien was right in subsequently singling out the story itself as the primary factor in the novel's success. He would also have been right, I think, in judging that his audience was enthralled by the consistency of his mythology. He was betraying modern thinking, however, when he confided that "it is, I suppose, some test of the consistency of a mythology as such, if it is capable of some sort of rational or rationalized explanation."[26]

In retrospect, it seemed to Tolkien that much of the myth represented a "creative error," as Christopher Tolkien put it, on the part of its maker.[27] For instance, he found the timing of "Narn I Hîn Húrin" (the Tale of the Children of Hurin) highly improbable. "A bare 400 years" since the dawn of the race of men, Tolkien objected, "is quite inadequate to produce the variety" found in mankind's gene pool at the time of Túrin.[28]

Tolkien did concede that "so great a work (in size) cannot be perfect."[29] Despite the beauty and grandeur of the story, however, Tolkien was able to assess as "astronomically absurd" his tale of the "making of the Sun and Moon." After all, he said, it is foolish to postulate the existence of the moon prior to the sun, and inconsistent with both science and experience to have the sun first rise in the west. "You can make up stories of that kind when you live among people who have the same general background of imagination," Tolkien said. However, he asserted, when it is "the general belief that we live upon a 'spherical' island in 'space' you cannot do this any more."[30] The fanciful nature of his fiction, Tolkien began to feel, was its own worst enemy.

In evaluating the various revisions which Tolkien attempted in order to reconcile some of this "absurdity" with the "facts" of modern science, Christopher Tolkien agreed with his father's hindsight. "How can it be acceptable," the younger Tolkien asks, "that the Evening Star is the Silmaril cut by Beren from Morgoth's crown?" He continues: "The art of the 'Sub-creator' cannot, or should not attempt to, extend to the 'mythical' revelation of a conception of the shape of the Earth and the origin of the lights of heaven that runs counter to the known physical truths of his own days."[31]

Why not? Does the "sub-creator," as postulated by Tolkien, work in deference to and in praise of the "known physical truths of his own days"? Not at all. The sub-creator works in honor to, and for the glory of, the true

Creator; and just as the measure of the consistency and value of Christianity is not to be found in "rational" or "rationalized" explanations, neither must we determine the measure of the sub-creation by such standards. That Tolkien felt such a compulsion — in spite of his technological aversions and the tenets of his own theory — betrays his own susceptibility to modern thought.

Such rationality, of course, is entirely consistent with Tolkien's professional work as a philologist. One doesn't become a clerk at Oxford, much less a don, without something of a reputation as a consistent, even formidable, thinker. Tolkien's essay "On Fairy Stories," for only one example, propounds a rigorous theory which the writing of *The Lord of the Rings* tested.[32] Such mental rigor wouldn't be possible without the very powers of reason which modernity trumpets and lauds. "The keener and clearer is the reason," Tolkien himself says, "the better fantasy will it make."[33]

Obeisance to rationality, however, especially when it comes to art, has its costs. Tolkien was realist enough to concede that reconciliation of his mythology with accepted theories of cosmogony would not necessarily be advisable. "One loses, of course," he wrote, "the dramatic impact."[34] It is fortunate for the reading public, apparently, that Tolkien never successfully transformed his "Flat World" myths[35] to a "Round World" form. Nonetheless, Tolkien's art, though romantic in its origin, was clearly influenced by modern thought.

Having said that, it is by no means a "dismissal" of Tolkien if we acknowledge a modernist influence in his thinking. It's unavoidable; much as Tolkien disliked the effects of modernism, he couldn't avoid its influence any better than could we.

Tolkien is not alone in being dependent on many of the technological advancements of modern society for his living and survival, while simultaneously hating them. Anybody with a Geiger counter could see where things were headed by 1945, but that didn't turn folks into the Unabomber. For Tolkien, what Doman calls the "Technological Death Wish" was the genesis of his mythology; yet technology made its publication possible. Similarly, the "Technological Death Wish" fuels many of the inconsistencies of our own behavior. Yet we must always be conscious, and critical, of the interplay of our culture and our faith, lest we somehow blame our failures on someone other than ourselves. Tolkien, at the very least, was willing to take full responsibility for whatever he wrote.

A DIVINE GIFT

Of course, maybe this is the true conflict: not between modernism and post-modernism, or between modernism and pre-modernism; but between culture and faith. An anonymous writer once asked, "Do you know what makes man the most suffering of all creatures? It is that he has one foot in the finite, and the other in the infinite, and that he is torn between both worlds." And so we find Tolkien, like ourselves, struggling to strike the proper balance between the two. The theory behind Tolkien's work demonstrates a solid grounding in the rational finite, even if the story itself invokes and pays tribute to the infinite. And so, because this tension is fully evident in his work, we would be mistaken to interpret Tolkien's escapist literature as wholly anti-modern. We would also be mistaken to understand Tolkien as a purely modern writer.

Still, we are left to wonder: What motivated Tolkien to take the prodigious step of transforming his personal escape into a meaningful mythology for England? It might be easier to answer a similar question, one expressed in terms that a Gamgee would understand: what would motivate a Hobbit to turn the entire Shire into a garden? Upon his return from the east, Sam could have, after all, thrown all of his efforts into restoring only his own little corner of the Shire; but he didn't. He used the gift of Galadriel to heal his whole land.

Like Sam, Tolkien returned from a war to the home of his youth. Like Sam, he could see around him the need for healing. And like Sam, he did not return from the war merely feeling wounded, scarred or damaged; rather, he returned in possession of something highly precious: something which he believed had the power to heal his whole land. What Sam returned with was a tiny box of soil from Lórien; but it was not the box that was the gift, it was the soil it contained. What Tolkien returned with was a story; however, it was not the story that was the gift, but the faith therein contained. And like Sam, Tolkien saw the responsibility that comes with such a great gift. It must not be closed inside a box, nor hidden under a bushel. As Yeats observed, "In dreams begins responsibility."[36]

And so, if we acknowledge that Tolkien was attempting something far more significant than just telling a ripping good story; and if we recognize that his purpose went well beyond decrying the destructive influence of modern progress, we find that we are explicitly led to the issue of Tolkien's faith. Precisely what gift did he see the need to share? Surely we must be able to discern some true understanding of God's Kingdom tucked under the veneer of Tolkien's fiction. Does he have both feet firmly planted in the infinite, or in the finite? Or is there evidence that he is the most suffering of all creatures, because he is torn between the two?

Chapter Four

TOLKIEN'S FAITH

The release of New Line Cinema's live-action films based on *The Lord of the Rings* has prompted pundits to rather perfunctorily and rhetorically ask: Is popular consumption of Tolkien's fantastic depiction of magic healthy, for a Christian? The question, of course, is loaded. The answer depends on an understanding of the role of the magical in Tolkien's fiction, the role of the supernatural in one's own faith, and an apprehension of the relation of magic to the supernatural for Tolkien himself.

Christian readers at Hollywood Jesus seem to fall into four differing camps with regard to this question. Two of these four camps tend to justify their position based on anecdotal evidence. Many defenders of Tolkien will cite *The Lord of the Rings* as the book that led them to Christ while detractors will claim its influence led them away from Christ and into neo-paganism or Wicca. An entire book could be filled with such anecdotal testimonies. Yet circumstantial evidence weighs heavily on both sides, and brings us no nearer a conclusive assessment of the effects of fictional magic on a Christian's spiritual health — it all depends on who one chooses to listen to, or perhaps on who talks loudest.

The third and fourth camps eschew reliance on subjective experience for their opinions; defender and detractor alike seem to rely on very little, particularly reason. On the one hand, reactionary opponents (based largely on second-hand reports about Tolkien's books) rather quickly issue summary indictments and condemnation. Granted, one does not need to actually enter a brothel to know that it's not a healthy place for a Christian; but if one's Christian friends, acquaintances and even family members are flocking into a supposed brothel down the street, one might be wise to reconsider the supposition, especially in the absence of firsthand knowledge.

On the other hand are the glib fans who rather unthinkingly presume that, because they personally find nothing objectionable, no one else should either. Like their reactionary counterparts, this group tends to cite one authority or another in praise of Tolkien, but are generally unable to make a coherent argument in defense of their own position. The glib and reactionary alike lack an objective framework for reliable assessments, and the biases of all four groups are worth checking at the door.

INTENT AND ARTIFACT

Meaning well and doing well are two entirely different things. "When a book leaves your hands," Flannery O'Connor wrote, "it belongs to God. He may use it to save a few souls or to try a few others, but I think that for the writer to worry about this is to take over God's business."[1] Good advice for the writer, perhaps; but if O'Connor is right, the implication is that the author's responsibility ends with intent and execution. From there begins the reader's responsibility. Books don't offend people, O'Connor suggests; people offend *themselves*, by what they find mirrored in books.

There is merit to this Chestertonian view, in that it is consistent with the aims of Consecration Analysis; and also because it gives us a vocabulary for our analysis. "The excellence of a work of art," O'Connor felt, "consists in the artifact, not in the good intentions of the artist."[2] This paraphrase of Thomas Aquinas differentiates between intent and consumption: one may mean well, but still do poorly. The artist, therefore, is judged by *intent*. The *artifact* — the end product of the intent, the work itself — is judged on its own merits.

Consequently, if the analysis of the following chapters indicates that there are faults in *The Lord of the Rings*, it does not follow that we must find fault with Tolkien the man, or with his faith. This distinction between intent and artifact allows us to focus, for the remainder of this chapter, solely on the question of Tolkien's intent. By doing so, we will come near to the heart of Tolkien's faith; and we shall do so in a responsible manner, without the waters being muddied by our gut reactions to Tolkien's artifact.

However, analysis of Tolkien's intent may also give an indication of the potential value of Tolkien's words: are they really worth listening to? When the Apostle Paul was evangelizing Asia Minor, he found the people of Berea commendable precisely for their analytic abilities. Rather than blithely accepting Paul as an emissary from God, or relying on anecdotal evidence of the power of Paul's gospel, they "received the message with great eagerness and examined the Scriptures every day to see if what Paul said was true."[3]

The question of intent, then, becomes just as important for the reader as for the writer. Are we content, like the Thessalonians, to be agitated or merely entertained by what we read, without examining both the message and the messenger soberly? Or do we aspire to the "more noble" character of the Bereans?

Still, we must count the cost. The best advice I ever heard was a sermon in which the preacher said, "Know why you believe what you believe."[4] To do that, one must be absolutely unafraid. "Draw near to God," says the Scripture, "and God will draw near to you."[5] If we pursue God honestly, we must be prepared to come face to face with Him; and that prospect may be too terrifying for many, though it yields the greatest possible joy.

But who wouldn't be intimidated with the prospect of meeting God face to face? Only God Himself; and we are not God, and would do well to constantly remind ourselves of the fact. Until a Christian becomes truly Christlike, that Christian is spiritually impoverished, being so much less than what God desires or intends. But that just puts such a Christian in pretty good company: with the rest of the spiritually impoverished! Blessed are the poor in spirit, for they have plenty of brothers and sisters.

To a certain extent, calling oneself a Christian is like claiming to be a U.S. Treasury agent in Al Capone's Chicago: "Who would claim to be one, who was not?"[6] In assessing Tolkien's intent, we must approach our task with an advisable humility; for by claiming the name of Christ ourselves, we have declared ourselves imperfect without His grace. And so whatever standards we bring to bear upon J. R. R. Tolkien we must be willing to bring to bear upon ourselves.

For his part, Tolkien intended his work "to be consonant with Christian thought and belief."[7] What does that mean, precisely? What does "Christian" mean to a British Roman Catholic, after all? Or to an American Protestant? To an atheist? We may find clues by examining this claim against the central issue of the current fire-storm.

TOLKIEN, MAGIC AND WIZARDRY

Wizards are suddenly hot. In 1981, I saw John Boorman's *Excalibur* and was spectacularly numbed by the Authurian legend. Despite early, and memorable, performances by Gabriel Byrne, Liam Neeson and Patrick Stuart, it seemed that most audiences agreed: the whole wizard thing was just too dorky for words. Nigel Terry as King Arthur didn't help matters for post-Watergate post-Jimmygate cynics, of course; nor did memories of John Cleese's wizard "Tim" in *Monty Python and the Holy Grail* (1975). But suddenly, with the resurgence of interest in *The Lord of the Rings*, and the 21st century phenomenon called Harry Potter (among other entertainments), the concept of wizardry is once again fixed in the warp and weave of our cultural fabric. So questions have frequently been raised: how does "magic" figure into *The Lord of the Rings*, what did it mean to Tolkien, and what, exactly, are Tolkien's wizards?

Magic is an omnipresent feature of Tolkien's books. From Gandalf's perspective, some simple tricks of the wizard's trade can be found in his fireworks, or in his ability to provide light for the Fellowship as they pass through Moria. As correctly portrayed in Peter Jackson's movies, such ordinary magic passes pretty much without comment. It is natural, and expected. Gandalf is certainly capable of flamboyant demonstrations, however. One of which he is particularly proud is the flourish he adds to the flood which descends upon the Black Riders at the Ford of Bruinen. In the book, Elrond controls the waters of Bruinen (through the power of one of the rings crafted by Celebrimbor in ages past), but Gandalf magically adds the appearance of white stallions galloping amidst the foam.

Of what nature is such magic? Is it akin to the miracles performed by Jesus in the Bible, like raising Lazarus from the dead? Not at all. Nowhere in Tolkien's fiction does any created being have the power of life over death. In his letters, Tolkien explains frequently that the object of magic "is Art not Power."[8] It is the ability to apply knowledge of things as they truly are in such a way that they become transformed in the eyes of the uninitiated. Middle-Earth's fireworks are a perfect example: *magic* to Hobbits, but perfectly understandable to a modern audience. The mithril-inlaid gates of Moria are another: the product of the elevated craft of the Dwarves and Elves, but one whose secret has simply been lost. Were the same craft exercised for the purpose of dominion over others or personal advancement, it might well be called *technology* rather than *magic*. In our own world, such misuse might be equated with "attempting to conquer Sauron with the Ring," as Tolkien put it. "The penalty is, as you will know, to breed new Saurons, and slowly turn Men and Elves into Orcs."[9]

Man's proclivity for abuse of craft (think of Boromir's temptation, the biblical Tower of Babel, or the atomic bomb) relegates magic almost exclusively to the domain of wizards and Elves, in Tolkien's world. There is no possibility of mistaking a wizard for a human, or discovering that one has magical powers, as in the Harry Potter books. In Middle-Earth, magic is idealized, "an inherent power not possessed or attainable by Men as such."[10] A man may act under the influence of magic, but not, properly speaking, "do" magic.

One exception in Middle-Earth would be human practitioners of "'magic' traditions" of "secret cults" founded by corrupt wizards in the East;[11] another would be certain ecstatic utterances, such as the strange Elvish words that fall from Frodo's lips in the dark of Shelob's lair: "*Aiya Eárendil Elenion Ancalima!*"[12] As Tolkien says, "Those under special Elvish influence might call on the angelic powers for help in immediate peril or fear of evil enemies."[13] The effects of such influence are literally extraordinary, and not characteristic of a "natural" human experience. While Tolkien never publicly commented on the biblical gift of speaking in tongues, it is likely that he would have understood Frodo's episode (and others of its kind) in a manner consistent with the early Christian doctrine. Frodo "was 'inspired' to make this invocation," Tolkien said, "in a language he did not know."[14]

Significantly, the kind of magical incantation which we may perceive in Peter Jackson's movies — such as Arwen's "words of power" at the Ford of Bruinen and the "words on the wind" that Saruman sends to control the weather at Caradhras — really don't appear in Tolkien's fiction. While the specific mechanisms of Middle-Earth's magical craft are never explicitly discussed, the casting of spells, as we normally conceive it, is not among them. Magic is not transformational in Tolkien's work. Nobody may be turned into a toad who is not already one. At the Hollin gate to Moria, for instance, Tolkien writes of Gandalf trying various spells to open the doors. They don't work because they're not the right one. This door needs one particular verbal key for its lock, and until it is spoken — *mellon* — it will remain shut.

Middle-Earth's magic is accomplished by manipulating the apparent nature of things which already are, not by what Tolkien called "vulgar devices."[15] Blinking, or twitching one's nose, cannot produce magic. *The Lord of the Rings* is not *Bewitched* or *I Dream of Jeannie*. In fact, one's magical powers in Middle-Earth are in direct proportion to one's proximity to the divine. Having once dwelt in the Blessed Land, the Elves are the sole wielders of true magic in Middle-Earth — aside from the Wizards, who are themselves divine.

Eru, the One, is the supreme being of Tolkien's fantastic universe. Under him are an order of created beings, the Ainur. Some of these, the Valar, are given the task of ordering and supervising the affairs of Arda (our Earth).

Others, lesser of the Ainur, follow and serve the Valar in their work in Arda: the Maiar. These beings are of a class commonly thought of as *angels* or *demons*. Sauron himself is a fallen Maiar, as are Balrogs and other evil spirit beings. Also among the Maiar are the Istari, the Wizards. So in Tolkien's world, a Wizard is not a human with supernatural powers; a Wizard is, in fact, a supernatural being.

Tolkien was apparently sensitive to public perception of magic in his novels, most likely because of his own religious convictions. In early drafts of *The Lord of the Rings*, for instance, Tolkien has Elrond refer to Sauron as "the Magician,"[16] interchangeably with "Necromancer." All such references were removed in later drafts, to avoid unpleasant and controversial confusion. As we have seen, Tolkien's presentation of magic is different in nature from popular (and contemporary) notions of magic. What Dale Chihuly does with glass, for instance, might be considered a modern expression of Tolkien's magic; as might be the spell cast by the creation of Middle-Earth itself. After all, as Tolkien the philologist reminds us, the word "*spell* means both a story told, and a formula of power over living men."[17]

GODS, ANGELS AND THE TRINITY

A detailed discussion of wizards leads, however, as we have seen, to the potentially troubling subject of Tolkien's pantheon. Okay; so Gandalf, as a Wizard of Middle-Earth, is one of the Maiar. That means he is also one of the lesser Ainur; does that mean he is a god? Or is he an angel? Neither? What is the exact nature of the divine in Middle-Earth? And if we talk about *gods*, does that preclude *God*? The correct answer to these questions lies in Tolkien's intent, not our reactionary response to his words.

First, we must be abundantly clear, and not make excuses for the fact, that Tolkien very much understood the Valar as gods. His invented characters refer to them as gods,[18] even as "mighty and holy,"[19] a description many Christians reserve for the Godhead alone. The words of Tolkien's characters reflect what the *characters* think, and not necessarily what *Tolkien* thinks, of course; and there is evidence of some sensitivity to the issue on Tolkien's part. In drafts of *The Lord of the Rings*, for instance, the Hobbit Trotter (an early prototype for Strider) refers to "the land of the Gods and the Blessed Realm of Valinor."[20] Such "religious" references were purged from the text (along with Trotter!) by the time of the novel's publication.

However, such nomenclature for the Valar falls not only from the lips of Tolkien's characters; it also falls from the lips of the author. In letters and commentaries, both Tolkien and his son Christopher refer to the Valar as "gods."[21] When Tolkien does so, however, he uses the word in a way which may be foreign to us; that is, Tolkien distinguishes between "gods" and "God." Specifically, the gods of Middle-Earth are a certain class of "angelic beings."[22]

Webster's defines *archangel* as an "angel of high rank."[23] So when Tolkien describes the Maiar as "of the same order as the Great but of less might and majesty,"[24] we can see that, in essence, the Valar correspond to archangels and the Maiar correspond to angels. The term "gods" is used by Tolkien to correlate these classes of angelic beings to the deities of the Greek, Roman and Norse pantheons (among others).

Ignoring the perhaps astonishing discovery that Gandalf is essentially an angel, there are aspects to Tolkien's conception of these beings worthy of examination. First, literary critics have often pointed out that Tolkien's faith included the notion of guardian angels. While readers unfamiliar with the doctrine may consider it quaint, antiquated or heretical, Tolkien understands guardian angels as real, and as neither intercessory nor diminutive. They are not "a thing interposed between God and the creature," Tolkien wrote in a letter to Christopher, "but God's very attention itself, personalized."[25] The notion serves as a practical way to understand how God can literally pay attention to every single human being. Think of the messengers who visit Abraham and Lot, for instance; or the being which accompanied Daniel's three friends in Babylon's furnaces.

Second, and rather more significantly, Tolkien commented that the "Valar (angels) shared in" the making of Middle-Earth.[26] Protestants are especially keen in quoting the first chapter of the Gospel of John, which states that all things came into being through "the Word." The Word is Christ; and of course, Christ is God. So is Tolkien's conception of the creation at odds with Christian doctrine?

Well, the Bible never proposes any formal explanation for *how* Christ was the agent of creation; and the metaphor of Christ as the Word is intended to mirror the Genesis account of God speaking creation into existence. Since it is theologically conceivable that the creation of the angels predated the existence of the world, it is at least artistically plausible to postulate that the angels assisted in the work in some fashion.

In fact, Genesis is clear that the angels were perhaps *too* willing to assist. Many theologians understand the "sons of God" who intermarry with the "daughters of men" in the sixth chapter of Genesis[27] as willful, wayward angelic beings. Such an understanding would be consistent with the conduct of Tolkien's Ainur. Melian, for instance, weds

Thingol, an Elf; and their offspring, Lúthien, is an ancestor of both Aragorn and Arwen. The Ainur *and* biblical angels are creative, indeed; perhaps in a fashion, as Doman says, "unnervingly similar to the gods of Mount Olympus."[28] Tolkien, however, understood the Ainur as participants in the making of the world "only on the same terms as we 'make' a work of art or story."[29] Again, for Tolkien, it's about Art, not Power.

As Christian readers, we might also take offense to Tolkien's use of the word *divine* with respect to the Ainur. Many reserve this word for the Godhead, just as we often do the words *mighty* and *holy*. It's highly likely, however, that we are overly territorial about such words. Doman offers the following insight. "One reason Tolkien may do this so freely," she says, "is because Catholics constantly are turning to agents between themselves and God, something that I have noticed worries our [Protestant] Christian brethren very much. We have guardian angels, saints, relics, the Virgin Mary, liturgy, statues, prayer cards, fancy buildings, Popes, bishops, priests, nuns; and deeper in, the Eucharist, which to the outside observer seems like just another symbol, but which the Catholics believe is really the Lord, Jesus Christ Himself."[30] As we have seen with respect to guardian angels, Tolkien did not consider these things substitutionary intercessors, but as the immediate representative presence of the Almighty Himself.

This is an important point to remember, for the issue at hand is understanding Tolkien's faith, not forcing the square peg of Tolkien's beliefs into the round hole of our own theological presumptions. While we may be unfamiliar with Tolkien's broad understanding of God's direct intercession, for Tolkien it was essential. So we may need to proceed cautiously. Protestants tend to be critical of this aspect of Catholicism, in particular, as they tend to see

Christ and His Spirit as the only necessary mediators between themselves and God; hence the emphasis on a "personal" relationship with Jesus.

On the other hand, one anonymous Hollywood Jesus correspondent wrote that she had "lost her faith" because she felt her church was putting *Jesus* "in the way" of her relationship with God! There's obviously a wide range of thought about this among Christians. "So Tolkien could write of the Valar as 'divine,'" Doman continues, "and never wonder about whether or not he was on heretical grounds. And it wouldn't bother his Catholic readers either."[31] For Tolkien, the Ainur are "Divine" merely because they "were originally 'outside' and existed 'before' the making of the world."[32] Hence they share in the ordained "right to power (as distinct from its possession)."[33]

So where does this leave Eru? Is Eru Middle-Earth's God? Is Eru God Himself? If the Ainur are angelic beings, we can easily see that there is no true pantheon here, not even an hierarchical one. The theology of Middle-Earth is strictly monotheistic. Even the power of Eru is expressed in very Christian terms. For instance, Eru is not bound by the Ainur's knowledge of him or his will. He has the power to intervene in Middle-Earth, introducing new "things directly, which were not in the Music and so are not achieved through the Valar."[34] Thus Eru is transcendent.

Eru is also the father of Middle-Earth, as evidenced by Tolkien's consistent reference to the peoples and races of Middle-Earth as the children of Eru. And it is in this relation that we can finally see that, for Tolkien, Eru is the being we call God. For Tolkien, the Elves are the "Children of God" themselves.[35] While this may be repugnant to our own religious sensibilities, for Tolkien it was not. In fact "the 'gods' of higher mythology" should not be an obstacle, Tolkien claimed, to "a mind that believes in the Blessed Trinity."[36] So in Tolkien we find a believer in orthodox theology.

FAIRY STORIES AND SANCTIFICATION

I recently posed the following question to my wife: "If you knew you were going to be leaving soon for a long-term mission trip and were going to be thrown in with a complete stranger for the duration; and further, if you only had ten minutes to determine whether you could really harness yourself with this other believer to do God's work, what would you consider the most important thing to find out?" After thinking about it for a bit, Jenn responded: "Actually I would probably ask the other person what he would most like to know about *me*. That would be the surest way to find out what his spiritual priorities were."

Very wise advice. I'm sure that almost all of the folks in my local congregation, for instance, have a fairly orthodox understanding of the Trinity; but with how many of them would I really find it effective to minister intensively? Most of them, it seems, have different priorities than I do, choosing to expend a great deal of spiritual capital on issues like the "hymns vs. choruses" debate, budget crises, garage sales and caucuses. More power to them, if they are so called by God; but I am not likely, I must confess, to partner with these folks in ministry myself, except in a casual way. Such issues are only distantly related to my own calling.

So identifying the beliefs we *share* places us all squarely within God's Kingdom; but naming our own peculiar God-given passion within the church gives a good indication of how closely God intends for us to align ourselves with our brothers and sisters. It's a legitimate question, when approaching Tolkien's fiction, to ask: "Okay, Tolkien was an orthodox believer, but what aspects of his faith really distinguish him from other believers? And how much of my own spiritual energy should I invest in *his* passions?"

Tolkien's first great passion, as observed earlier, was for "heroic legend on the brink of history": for myth and fairy-story, and their therapeutic ennobling effect. Novelist William Faulkner put it this way: "I believe that the human spirit will prevail forever. It is our privilege to help it endure by lifting people's hearts, by reminding them of Courage and Honor and Hope and Pride and Compassion and Pity and Sacrifice, which have been the glory of their past."[37] But this was not, as we might assume, a primarily secular passion for Tolkien; rather, it was his chosen means of expressing his passion for God.

As early as 1916, Tolkien had been a founding member of the "Tea Club and Barrovian Society," a literary group he believed was destined to "rekindle an old light in the world" and "testify for God and Truth."[38] How? Through creative expression. "The Holy Spirit," Tolkien later wrote, "seems sometimes to speak through a human mouth providing art, virtue and insight he does not himself possess."[39] And if "the chief purpose of life, for any one of us, is to increase according to our capacity our knowledge of God by all the means we have, and to be moved by it to praise and thanks"[40] we had best get to it, said Tolkien. Only by using our God-given talents and spiritual gifts to express that praise and thanks can we be true to God's purposes for our lives, sharing our faith in a way that will be meaningful to others. So Tolkien did precisely that.

By 1938, in fact, Tolkien had managed to articulate a formal theory for the artistic "effoliation and multiple enrichment of creation."[41] Required reading in many university literature courses, his essay "On Fairy Stories" was originally conceived as a lecture, and later published in *Tree and Leaf*. In a way, the essay served as a manifesto for the literary experiment called *The Lord of the Rings*. Many of the essay's central tenets are crucial in understanding the driving passion of Tolkien's faith.

The first of these tenets is the artist's role as "sub-creator." Art is the means by which "an enchanter's power" may "cause woods to spring with silver leaves and rams to wear fleeces of gold, and put hot fire into the belly of the cold worm," Tolkien says. "In such 'fantasy,' as it is called, new form is made; Faerie begins."[42] Such "sub-creation" does not substitute for or diminish the Creator; it pays tribute, says Tolkien. And so Tolkien can say, "Let the sun first rise in the West, and set again in the West." And it does. And Tolkien sees that it is good, for it is his creation.

Of course, says Tolkien, the mere creation of such "Secondary Worlds" is not in itself sufficient. The artist strives to create a world into which the "mind can enter" such that one may "believe it" while one is, "as it were, inside. The moment disbelief arises, the spell is broken; the magic, or rather art, has failed."[43] True sub-creation, according to Tolkien, reveals the "willing suspension of disbelief" to be a cheap imitation of the real thing: *Secondary Belief*. Though successful creation of a "credible, commanding" secondary belief "will certainly demand a special skill, a kind of Elvish craft,"[44] the alternative is not to suspend disbelief so much as to have it "hanged, drawn and quartered."[45]

The importance of effective sub-creation is tied to what Tolkien calls the literary function of Recovery, Escape and Consolation. While we are readily familiar with escapism, and have considered it previously in our discussion of Tolkien's driving motives, the concepts of Recovery and Consolation may require some elucidation. The former is perhaps best understood in Tolkien's affirmation that the themes of *The Lord of the Rings* lie not "in strife and war and heroism," but rather in "freedom, peace, ordinary life and good liking." These stirring virtues, Tolkien says, may "grow stale by custom and turn into the humdrum" without "the existence of a great world outside the Shire."[46] One reason God allows suffering, Tolkien suggests, is that good might be fully recognizable. Thus, the sub-creator may also strive to "clean our windows; so that the things seen clearly may be freed from the drab blur of triteness or familiarity."[47] Recovery may also be understood through the aphorism, "Absence makes the heart grow fonder." One way then, to provoke effective thinking about "whatever is true, whatever is noble, whatever is pure, whatever is lovely, whatever is admirable"[48] may be for the sub-creator to effectively remind us of "hunger, thirst, poverty, pain, sorrow, injustice, death."

Many instinctively recoil against such a notion. But Tolkien argues that a means of Recovery which might do violence to the propriety of our own private goodness and light may be necessary for Consolation. The very possibility, he says, of *dyscatastrophe* — a term coined by Tolkien to signify extreme sorrow and failure — is necessary to the "joy of deliverance."[49] And so the Consolation of *eucatastrophe* — also coined by Tolkien to signify the joy of deliverance — is not possible without an effective depiction of the alternative. Without the cross, he observes, there is no joy of resurrection.

This is not to say that Tolkien was after tragedy. A story like Hamlet derives its dramatic tension from the inevitability of the protagonist's demise. The plot turns on a fatal flaw which dooms Hamlet from the start. Drama, Tolkien argues, is fatalistic and by nature tragic. Tragedy, he insists, is the literary opposite of the "eucatastrophic" Fairy Story.[50] "Dyscatastrophe" is a means to an end, not the end in itself.

And this simple observation is at the heart of Tolkien's thesis. The artist's task is to awaken a desire for the Consolation of eucatastrophe, "satisfying it while often whetting it unbearably,"[51] as Tolkien said. This is what the artist was created by God to do; "we make still by the law in which we're made."[52] But not for the artist's honor; rather, to point to the cross: "The Resurrection is the eucatastrophe of the story of the Incarnation."[53] Through a tribute to the *evangelium*, the artist finds "that all his bents and faculties have a purpose, which can be redeemed."[54] The artist's "desire and aspiration of sub-creation has been raised to the fulfillment of Creation."[55]

The ideas put forward in Tolkien's essay were undoubtedly honed by the lively discussion of the Inklings, a loose affiliation of Christian Oxford dons who met with some regularity in C. S. Lewis' apartments during the latter part of the 1930s and into the 1940s. A shared belief in such ideas would lead Tolkien, Lewis and Charles Williams (most prominently, among others) to each write and publish notoriously successful works. The overtly Christian tone of Lewis' works is perhaps the most famous exponent, in part because of Lewis' prolific output of apologetics; and also in part because of his more mainstream English Protestant faith.

Tolkien, on the other hand, was a Catholic; and Roman Catholics were a distinct, persecuted religious minority in the United Kingdom for the better part of the 20th century. We should not be surprised to find Tolkien taking a lower-profile approach to sharing his faith, whether it was deliberate or unconscious. His approach was nevertheless extremely effective, as it was to a great degree a catalyst for Lewis' acceptance of Christ.

But Tolkien was not one of the "cultural Catholics" which many Protestants are only too eager to caricature and condemn. Tolkien's faith was not only lived out in a vibrant and unusually personal way, but also in pious observance of the more conventional hallmarks of the Roman orthodoxy. For Tolkien, the "Blessed Sacrament" was the "one great thing to love on earth."[56]

Non-liturgical Protestants are often hindered (to a lesser or greater degree, depending on which brand of Protestantism one buys) in their understanding of sanctification and consecration because of a preference for "ordinances" over "sacraments." For instance, in the sharing of communion my Christian Church brethren *symbolically* partake in the body and blood of Christ. My Roman Catholic friends, on the other hand, find in the Eucharist the actual, trans-substantiated blood and flesh of our Lord. Now, the merits of one doctrine over the other may be argued until the cows come home (even long afterward); but the Catholic doctrine is illustrative of a general tendency to see the power of God dynamically at work in the world around us. Obviously, we must be careful not to worship the sacraments themselves, instead of the God they honor. But Tolkien was deeply affected, in an apparently positive manner, by a religious world view which encourages a daily (if ritual) observance of God's ability to apply all things as "conduits of His grace" so that they are "sanctified by being agents of His action."[57]

THE CORN AND THE CHAFF

The sacramental view also plays into controversial Catholic teachings about Mary: How can one not be radically sanctified, one Catholic friend posits, by the procreative presence of the Holy Spirit in the womb? Again, though we might take issue with the doctrines of the Immaculate Conception or the Assumption, the issue at hand is not what we believe; the issue is what Tolkien believed, and how those beliefs affected the intent of his fiction. And Tolkien was passionate about his Marian devotion. When Tolkien remarked that *The Lord of the Rings* "is of course a fundamentally religious and Catholic work," one principal "religious element" that he felt had been "absorbed into the story and the symbolism" was "Our Lady, upon which all my own small perception of beauty both in majesty and simplicity is founded."[58]

The pervasive Marian symbolism in the novel is fully explicated by other writers; but the presence of "Our Lady" in the broader mythology is most directly manifested in Elbereth, one of the Valar. In the same way that Tolkien might have directed prayers to Mary, the Elves might compose a "hymn to Elbereth,"[59] or Sam might cry out, "*Gilthoniel, A Elbereth!*"[60] as he plunges past the Watchers of Cirith Gorgor.

While the Elbereth-Mary connection in *The Lord of the Rings* is more properly a subject for the body of our Consecration Analysis yet to come, it serves here as a bridge for examining the second dominant aspect of Tolkien's faith: the humility with which he approached his work. "A writer may be basically 'benevolent' according to his lights (as I hope I am) and yet not be 'beneficent' owing to error and stupidity," Tolkien wrote. In other words, a writer may be motivated by a desire to do good, and still do none.

> "I may be in error (at some or all points): my truths may not be true, or they may be distorted: and the mirror I have made may be dim and cracked. But I

should need to be fully convinced that anything I have 'feigned' is actually harmful, *per se* and not merely because misunderstood, before I should recant or rewrite anything."[61]

Are we as readers also willing to admit the possibility of error? Many expect far too little of our entertainments. Do others expect too much? While Catholics in general might appreciate Tolkien's Marian symbolism, many Protestants might be among those pressing Tolkien to "recant."

The merits or demerits of Catholic Marian devotion may be debated at length, but such wrangling over words would bring us no nearer an understanding of Tolkien's faith, which is the issue at hand. The fact remains, whether we agree with Catholic doctrine or not, that Tolkien was attempting to be true to the Christian faith *as he understood it* — and such piety is commendable. And the fact also remains that Tolkien freely admitted that his artistic expression of Christian truth may not have been perfect — and such humility is commendable.

So if we choose to take issue with Tolkien's fiction because it reflects objectionable doctrine, we have picked a fight with the wrong party. To expect that every disciple of Christ will come to personal conclusions about every theological debate, on the scale of Aquinas' *Summa Theologica,* is unreasonable. It just doesn't happen. Yet while we're going about balancing our checkbooks, boiling cabbage and waxing our cars, there are a handful of folks who really do devote themselves to that level of doctrinal understanding. And we might do well — as did Tolkien — to consider their opinions with a certain measure of respect instead of the disdain with which they are sometimes met.

Continued spiritual growth must lead, at some point, to letting go of knowing, and focusing more on being. The

Bereans, for instance, still managed to treat Paul with respect while they went about examining his words against Scripture. Tolkien's piety was a model of such humility. He was not fixed on being "right" about his faith, only consistent in the practice of what he had every reason to believe was doctrinally sound; and if a critic were to take issue with his work, Tolkien would demand that the critic demonstrate his work wrong or harmful, not just problematic. The critic must be humble, too. "Only one's Guardian Angel, or indeed God Himself," Tolkien wrote, "could unravel the real relationship between personal facts and an author's works."[62]

Tolkien expected his work to be problematic, however: He knew it to be the product of human effort, not holy writ. "What thousands of grains of good human corn must fall on barren and stony ground, if such a very small drop of water should be so intoxicating," Tolkien wrote to his son. "Do you think 'The Ring' will come off, and reach the thirsty?"[63] he asked, wondering about *The Lord of the Rings'* potential for achieving effective "Consolation." Jesus' metaphor of the sowing of seed was perhaps Tolkien's favorite for understanding the nature of his life's work.

In "The Dialog of Finrod and Andreth" we find what may be the latest original tale in Tolkien's mythology — and one of the most important. In the Dialog, the Elvish King Finrod debates the fate of men with Andreth, a human loremaster. During the course of their conversation, Finrod explains to Andreth that the surety of Elvish faith is based on direct contact with the Valar. She responds that the human Wise

"do not speak with assurance or with one voice, having no sure knowledge such as ye boast of, but perforce depending upon 'lore,' from which truth (if it can be found) must be winnowed. And in every winnowing there is chaff with the corn that is chosen, and doubtless some corn with the chaff that is rejected."[64]

Finrod also observes that "it may often happen that friends and kinsmen see some things plainly that are hidden from their friend himself."[65] So Tolkien knows that his mythology may contain both chaff and corn of which he is unaware, and he also knows that the reader's winnowing of his corn may also be prone to error. It's only natural. "Beware of the chaff with your corn, Andreth,"[66] warns Finrod.

We may be after seeds of truth in winnowing Tolkien's lore; but Tolkien advises both winnowing *and* a cautious consumption of what is winnowed. Tolkien knows that human imperfection "makes our devices not only fail of their desire but turn to new and horrible evil. So we come inevitably from Daedalus and Icarus to the Giant Bomber."[67] Wings to fly, yes; but to what purpose?

Pride and humility are also addressed in "Of Aulë and Yavanna," one of Tolkien's earliest tales and one which survived virtually unchanged. The story recounts Aulë's creation of the Dwarves. This hardy folk were not a part of the Music of the Ainur, and therefore did not spring from the mind of Eru-Ilúvatar. Instead, Aulë, driven by his desire to create a people of his own, fashions the Dwarves from the stuff of the earth; but because they did not originate in the mind of Eru, they have no will of their own, and are entirely reliant on Aulë. Eru chastises Aulë for his presumptuousness in assuming the role of creator, and vows to destroy the Dwarves; but he eventually recants after Aulë demonstrates remorse for his wrongdoing.

In this story, as in the Dialog, we find Tolkien's acknowledgment of the problem of subcreation. If even one of the Ainur (two, if we count Melkor) shows initiative outside that directed by Eru, then subcreation may sometimes cross the line from tribute into blasphemy due to pride or the inevitable conflict of free will.

There is no doubt that the urge to create is God-given, for it is one of His characteristics; and we are made in His image. But through Aulë's indiscretion, Tolkien makes it clear that unrestrained subcreation becomes as much a problem of hubris as an expression of homage. "Akallabêth," Tolkien's tale of man's corrupt and prideful assault on the land of the gods, tells the same tale.

"Every finite creature must have some weakness," Tolkien writes. "It is not sinful when not willed, and when the creature does his best (even if it is not what should be done) as he sees it — with the conscious intent of serving Eru."[68] But one *may* sin, Tolkien implies, if one's weakness becomes willful, or if one does not do one's best; or if one acts in service to someone or something other than God.

Tolkien himself, then, affirms that the intentions of the artist are crucial; and as a Christian artist, he believes that he is truly trying to accomplish something worthy of his calling. And in consecration analysis it is by the intention that we judge the artist. He also affirms that the artifact is to be judged by what it actually is: corn, chaff, or some mixture of the two. And if there is some weakness in the artifact itself, which is to be expected since none is wholly good but God,[69] that's okay. There's no sin in that, or blame to be laid, unless the reader approaches the work with deliberately ill intent; or if the reader misapprehends the work because of willful ignorance.

Tolkien's work is not itself Truth, nor purported to

be. Some winnowing is required to discern Truth. And there is a great deal of corn there; and hopefully, to the discerning Christian, some chaff also. Everyone, and perhaps especially the Christian, needs to be more discerning about what is consumed, whether it's from Tolkien, the Trinity Broadcasting Network, or the pulpit. Of course, the most dangerous chaff is not someone else's, but your own.

THE FALLEN WORLD AND HUMAN HOPE

"Men have a strange power for good or ill, and for things aside from the purpose of the Valar or of Elves," says one of Tolkien's more obscure characters. "And their joy is small, which should be great."[70] The reason that this is so in Middle-Earth as well our own world is the same: the Fall.

"The essence of a *fallen* world is that the *best* cannot be attained," Tolkien explained in a letter to his son Michael, "but by denial and suffering. Faithfulness in Christian marriage," he goes on to illustrate, "entails that: great mortification. For a Christian man there is *no escape*. Marriage may help to sanctify & direct to its proper object his sexual desire; its grace may help him in the struggle; but the struggle remains. It will not satisfy him — as hunger may be kept off by regular meals."[71] All have sinned, Tolkien affirms, and fall well short of the glory of God; and our brokenness affects everything we do: "in the individual lives of all but a few, the balance is debit — we do so little that is positive good, even if we negatively avoid what is actively evil."[72]

Tolkien's understanding of "corn and chaff" comes as a direct consequence of his conviction of the world's fallenness. It comes as no surprise that Tolkien said his life's work was "mainly concerned with Fall, Mortality, and the Machine"[73] as there "cannot be any 'story' without a Fall — all stories are ultimately about the Fall."[74]

Frodo's tragic failure at Orodruin is illustrative of the effects of the Fall, as Tolkien saw it. Ordinarily good, faithful and true, Frodo was confronted with one of those "abnormal situations," as Tolkien put it, which "demand a strength of mind and body which he does not possess: he is in a sense doomed to failure, doomed to fall to temptation."[75] He clutches at the Ring and claims it for himself because it is "possible for the good, even the saintly, to be subjected to a power of evil which is too great for them to overcome — in themselves."[76]

Such an acknowledgment, for Tolkien, is not an excuse to lay blame, however. It is merely one aspect of providence: "the power of Evil in the world is *not* finally resistible by incarnate creatures, however 'good'"[77] because "Grace is not infinite, and for the most part seems in the Divine economy limited to what is sufficient for the accomplishment of the task appointed."[78] Frodo was meant to fail, Tolkien argues, so that Eru's purposes could be understood to prevail not through the righteousness of the Ringbearer, but through the sanctifying work of mercy: Bilbo's and Frodo's decisions to spare Gollum's life. Our God is best able to deliver us, in the end, not if we are perfect but if we strive to be faithful to Him all along the way.

Still, even our appreciation of providence and God's omnipotence is tarnished by our fallenness. "Our whole nature at its best and least corrupted, its gentlest and most humane, is still soaked with the sense of 'exile,'" Tolkien writes. "As far as we can go back, the nobler part of the human mind" is not only conscious of Eden, but also consumed "with the thought of its loss. We shall never recover it."[79]

Tolkien's wartime letters and the entire setting of *The Lord of the Rings*, written mostly between 1938 and

1945, are steeped with "the heart-wracking sense of the vanished past."[80] The horror of the first half of the 20th century, which banished forever the promised glow of the Enlightenment, weighed heavily on Tolkien's faith. Even with the return of the king to Middle-Earth, hope — *Estel*, Aragorn's Elvish name — is limited: long live the king, yes; but not forever.

Tolkien was not alone, of course. The same wartime pessimism was also pervasive on the west side of the Atlantic. "When the German juggernaut rolled over Europe for the second time in his adult life," Tarkington's biographer observed, "his optimistic faith in man's destiny was shaken, and he conceded that 'the future has never seemed more uncertain or dangerous.'"[81]

After World War II was well over, Tolkien explicitly revisited the subject of Hope in "The Dialog of Finrod and Andreth." The Dialog is perhaps the latest original addition to Tolkien's mythology (1959 at the earliest), and is accompanied by a detailed commentary almost as long as the Dialog itself. It was apparently crucial to Tolkien, at such a late date, to clarify the nature of hope for the men of Middle-Earth.

Because man is "born to life everlasting, without any shadow of any end,"[82] says Andreth in the Dialog, no "heart of man is content" in this life.[83] When Finrod suggests that passing from this life in death should not then be feared, but seem "as a release, or return, nay! as going home," [84] Andreth cannot agree. Even a pure soul, separated from the corrupt body, would be incomplete: Eru's original gift to man was incorruptibility of the conjoined body and soul; and the Fall has marred that forever. "What is hope?" Andreth asks, somewhat rhetorically. "An expectation of good, which though uncertain has some foundation in what is known? Then we have none."[85]

Finrod replies by making distinctions between *hope* as men define it — what Tolkien described in 1956 as "hope without guarantees"[86] — and *estel*, or hope as the Elves define it: trust "not defeated by the ways of the world, for it does not come from experience, but from our nature and first being." What Finrod posits is a nearly Christian faith, a confidence that Eru (God) "will not suffer Himself to be deprived of His own, not by any Enemy, not even by ourselves."[87] Eru demands "two things from His Children," Tolkien observed in his commentary on the Dialog: "belief in Him, and proceeding from that, hope or trust in Him."[88] And our human trust, or faith, is bolstered by God's miraculous interventions, which we tend to perceive as "intrusions (as we say, erring) into real or ordinary life," as Tolkien put it; "but they do intrude into real life"[89] in dynamic and indisputable ways.

If Tolkien, as a devout believer had confidence that there "is a place called 'heaven' where the good here unfinished is completed,"[90] then it is not surprising that he should culminate the Dialog's discussion of hope with an eschatological vision. His earliest mythologies had always included prophecies of the "Second Music of the Ainur."[91] The future promised a time when the disruptive themes of Melkor should be remedied and "the themes of Ilúvatar be played aright" because "all shall then understand his intent in their part, and shall know the comprehension of each."[92] Or, as the Apostle Paul put it, a time when we shall know even as we have been fully known.[93]

But in the Dialog, Tolkien goes beyond visions of a new heaven and new earth; he introduces, for the first time in the history of his mythology, a messianic prophecy:

The One will himself enter into Arda, and heal Men and all the Marring from the beginning to the end. This [the Wise] say also, or they feign, is a rumor that has come down through years uncounted, even from the days of our undoing.[94]

Finally, at the very end of the development of Middle-Earth's mythology, a hope which does not disappoint — *estel:* faith — is introduced. Tolkien's prophetic eschatological vision is as explicit as any to be found in Genesis or Isaiah. Still, Finrod realizes that until the coming of Eru into Arda, the faith of Andreth and her people will suffer. Only the Incarnation itself, unwriteable for Tolkien, will provide true consolation. Men will have no peace until the prophecy is fulfilled.

As early as 1944, Tolkien could assert the value of acting in good conscience. "If you cannot achieve inward peace, and it is given to few to do so (least of all to me) in tribulation," he wrote, "do not forget that the aspiration for it is not a vanity, but a concrete act."[95] Articulation of the distinction between mere hope and true faith in the Dialog may have led to later clarity. "Though the 'absolute ideal' may be 'unattainable'" in this life, he wrote in 1963, "to ourselves we must present the absolute ideal without compromise, for we do not know our own limits of natural strength (+grace), and if we do not aim at the highest we shall certainly fall short of the utmost that we could achieve." Though we may be "finite creatures with absolute limitations upon the powers of our soul-body structure in either action or endurance," he goes on to say, "*moral* failure can only be asserted, I think, when a man's effort or endurance falls *short* of his limits."[96]

This is a more hopeful moderation of his darker wartime views. It is not the inevitable triumph of evil that dooms us to failure, then; it is our own lack of perseverance. The walk of faith which led Tolkien to this conclusion was remarkable: from the Tea Club and Barrovian Society, on the battlefields of France, to the meetings of the Inklings, against the final disillusionment of World War II, through the writing of *The Lord of the Rings* itself, and in the terrific witness to God's power which continues even after his death.

A DARK INFLUENCE

At the time of the publication of *The Lord of the Rings*, however, Tolkien was still plagued by a seeming spiritual ambivalence. At that time, he could assert that his faith had increased "as a development of my own thought on my own life and work (technical and literary)." He no longer felt "either ashamed or dubious of the Eden 'myth.'"[97] Still, he could simultaneously feel that his writing might be "just a fruitless private hobby."[98]

Naturally, this darkness worked its way into his writing. "I am a Christian, and indeed a Roman Catholic," he wrote to Amy Ronald, "so that I do not expect 'history' to be anything but a 'long defeat'."[99] As he was working on the most visible passages of his mythology, Tolkien's world was unfortunately one, outside the sacraments, in which God's spiritual influence had seemingly withdrawn as an active intercessory good. This was a darkness fully evident to his close friend: "The War of the Ring is only one of a thousand wars" against Satan, C. S. Lewis wrote. "Every time we win we shall know that our victory is impermanent. If we insist on asking for the moral of [Tolkien's] story, that is its moral: a recall from facile optimism and wailing pessimism alike, to that hard, yet not quite desperate, insight into Man's unchanging predicament."[100]

Chapter Five

A CONSECRATED LORD OF THE RINGS

So, what makes a book a Christian book? Or, to ask the question more broadly, what makes art Christian art? Perhaps that's a trick question. After all, Christian music is what they play on Christian radio stations, and Christian books are what they sell in Christian book stores, right? Well, yes... and no.

It's true that certain radio stations and book stores (even book distributors) focus on art that's specifically targeted at a Christian audience. But it's also true that you can buy Bibles at Borders, and most of the titles listed by Christian Book Distributors (CBD) can be found on *Amazon.com*. And the latest *Left Behind* book or *Veggie Tales* DVD is also likely to be on sale at the local supermarket.

But Christians tend to be suspicious of music, books and movies available at mainstream outlets. The work of Tim LaHaye and Phil Vischer might only be exceptions to the rule: Christian works which have become so popular that they are "cross-over" successes. However (the logic goes), *Left Behind*, *Veggie Tales* and even Amy Grant debuted in Christian book stores; and *The Omega Code* wasn't produced in Hollywood.

The label *Christian*, then, when applied to art, often has more to do with point of origin and point of purchase than actual content. To a certain extent, this is natural, and good. After all, when we're looking for faith-related reading, it's convenient to go to the local "Family Christian Bookstore"; and when we're after the latest Tom Clancy potboiler, we head to Barnes and Noble. Convenient labels are precisely that: convenient, and we live in a convenience-oriented culture.

It's also comforting to know that someone is minding the farm for us, that the publishers have more or less shouldered the burden of making sure the stuff stocked on the shelves of Christian bookstores actually *is* Christian. If it weren't safe to consume, we wouldn't find it there, right?

To a degree, yes. But an inability to find a book on those same shelves does not necessarily mean it's unsafe. Regardless of where a book came from originally, or where it was bought, it is likely to have high proportions of what Tolkien referred to as "corn" *and* "chaff." And the consumer is *never* absolved of the responsibility of discernment. Judgment about whether any given work is Christian or not — including *The Lord of the Rings* — will likely be determined by how the judge defines *Christian;* and our denominational differences alone tell us that alternate definitions abound and vary widely.

ALLEGORY AND EASY ANSWERS

So we find ourselves once again in the same quandary as the disciples: in the absence of reliable, convenient labels, how do we know who is with Jesus, and how do we know who is against him? Can we dismiss *The Lord of the Rings* because it's not found on the shelves of Christian bookstores? Or must we endorse it simply because it was written by a Christian author? Neither, actually, if we don't demand easy answers.

In our proposed model of Consecration Analysis, it is incumbent upon us to first determine intent; and this involves both the author's stated purposes (which we have reviewed in great detail in the previous chapter) as well as the purposes which we find expressed in the work itself.

Hence, we now approach *The Lord of the Rings* and ask: Was Tolkien successful in honoring and glorifying Christ in his novel? What corn do we find, and what chaff? And is it Tolkien's own chaff that we find, or the chaff that we tracked into the threshing floor on the soles of our own shoes?

In answering these questions, we know what we will *not* find in *The Lord of the Rings:* Allegory. Books like *Left Behind* are seemingly easy to assess because characters explicitly talk about Jesus, God and the Holy Spirit; and recognizable Biblical events abound. In more fantastic fiction, finding references to the persons of the Trinity may be difficult; C. S. Lewis' *Narnia* books, however, have become a sort of "gold standard" for such fiction. Why? Because by design they are an extended (if not entirely consistent) allegory, with Aslan as the Christ-figure. The Christian reader can clearly see the parallels: Aslan is the agent of creation; he is the substitutionary sacrifice for sin; and he rises victoriously and powerfully from the dead.

In *The Lord of the Rings*, however, allegories are not present, and cannot properly (in a literary sense) be explicated. Why? Because Tolkien despised allegory and deliberately avoided it in his work. The conclusion to be drawn is that Middle-Earth is no Narnia. Okay, that's pretty obvious; but it also doesn't have to be, and wasn't intended to be. It's no crime, either, since the presence of allegory is not what makes a fictional work Christian (if anything in particular does). Allegory did not originate with C. S. Lewis; in fact, it did not originate with Christians at all. Allegory cannot be held up as the only legitimate form of Christian homage.

So why are analysts so given to finding allegory in *The Lord of the Rings*? Tolkien addressed this question himself, observing "that the better and more closely woven a story is the more easily can those so minded find allegory in it."[1] People find allegory in his work, Tolkien says, not because he put it there, but because his work is good, and folks want to find allegory there. Again, this reinforces the observation that sifting corn and chaff is a dicey business and prone to error.

Apart from Tolkien's dislike of allegory, however, is another complicating factor. Were Tolkien prone to writing allegory, what subject for allegory would one find in his stories? Not the Christ. The "Incarnation of God," Tolkien confessed, "is an infinitely greater thing than anything I would dare to write."[2] Such a topic, Tolkien felt, was an inappropriate subject for his fiction.

So if we can't find an allegory for Christ in *The Lord of the Rings*, what may we find there? A wealth of symbolism; a smattering of Biblical allusions; and dominant strains of Christian themes. Symbols and allusions, of course, may be more apparent (and easily confused with allegory), so we will discuss some of the more obvious of these first; then move on to the themes found beneath the surface of Tolkien's story.

SYMBOLS AND ALLUSIONS

> *From the ashes a fire shall be woken,*
>
> *A light from the shadows will spring;*
>
> *Renewed shall be blade that was broken,*
>
> *The crownless again shall be king.*[3]

Thus concludes the prophetic verse belonging to Aragorn. In biblical prophecy, the fire, the light, the sword and the crown are the Messiah's; and the title of the third volume of *The Lord of the Rings* — *The Return of the King* — not only betrays the climax of the story. It also reinforces the novel's most obvious Christological symbolism. Aragorn is recognized by Gondor's nurse Ioreth as the king foretold in prophetic words about "the hands of a healer."[4] He returns beyond hope from the Paths of the Dead, "preaching to the lost," so to speak, at the Black Stone of Erech; his armies are victorious over his foes; and through victory he claims his long-awaited bride and ascends the throne to claim his rightful place in the hearts of men. The King has returned, as foretold in prophecy, and during his reign he truly becomes a Prince of Peace.

Even before the final victory, Aragorn's ascendancy is foretold. At the crossroads, Frodo sees the flowers growing on the brow of the fallen head of the statue, and observes, "The King has got a crown again."[5] Earlier, in Ithilien with Faramir, Frodo and Sam learn much of the history of the Stewards of Gondor. The tale is reminiscent of the language used by Jesus in teaching about the Kingdom of God in Matthew 24: "Who then is that faithful and wise steward, whom his lord shall make ruler over his household, to give them their portion of meat in due season? Blessed is that servant, whom his lord when he cometh shall find so doing."[6] Even in those around Aragorn we find potent symbols pointing to the Christ.

But Aragorn does not function as an allegorical figure. He is not the agent of creation; he is not God incarnate, born of a virgin; he does not die and actually return from the dead. In fact, his is not even the greatest sacrifice to be found in the story. Neither is Aragorn the only figure in the story in whom Christ-like glimpses can be found.

Consider Gandalf: In the mines of Moria, we find the first chinks in his armor. Following the confrontation with the unknown power in the Chamber of Records, he remarks, "Ah! I have never felt so spent, but it is passing."[7]

Gandalf? Physically taxed by the use of his powers? And then he falls into darkness in his death struggle with the Balrog, saving the lives of the Fellowship! What is this madness? How can such strength exhibit such weakness? Or *is* it weakness? In a similar way, Jesus feels a dissipation of power when working miracles (see Luke 8:46), and Himself dies on the cross to save others.

Later, Gimli and Legolas, along with Aragorn, enter Fangorn with much foreboding. But it is here that they encounter a changed, reborn Gandalf. A great victory seems to have come through death. But did Gandalf really die? The most direct statement that he makes is, "I have passed through fire and deep water."[8] He also states that he was "sent back,"[9] and warns that, despite his victory over the Balrog and his increased powers in passing from Grey to White, "black is mightier still."[10] But Aragorn rejoins, "We have One, mightier than they: the White Rider. He has passed through the fire and the abyss, and they shall fear him. We will go where he leads."[11] Tolkien's choice to capitalize *One* here is telling, as is Shadowfax's similarity to the White Horse of Revelation.

Also consider Frodo. Below Rauros, beyond the twin images of Isildur and Anárion, atop Amon Hen, he confronts an enormous choice: to take the Ring to Gondor and the War, or to take the Ring to Mordor and certain destruction. Like Boromir, he carries with him his own temptation, the desire to take "the way that seems easier."[12] Frodo is Everyman, and (as the writer of Hebrews says of Christ) is "tempted in every way, just as we are."[13] Every day, we are confronted with the decision of Olivet, the choice between the easy way out and what we know is right. "Wide is the gate and broad is the road that leads to destruction," Jesus said, "but small is the gate and narrow the road that leads to life, and only a few find it."[14]

We even find *anti*-Christ symbolism in *The Lord of the Rings*. The Fellowship of the Nine Walkers, to cite only one example, sets out southward from Rivendell. They depart at night, to avoid the watchful eyes of Sauron's spies; but Boromir rashly blasts the horn of Gondor, for which he earns a reprimand from Elrond. Boromir replies, "I will not go forth as a thief in the night."[15] This is an interesting choice of words to put in Boromir's mouth. Aragorn has already been identified as the one about whom the prophecies speak, the heir of Isildur; so the setting forth of the Fellowship, is, in a way, the beginning of the return of the king. And in New Testament prophecy, Jesus compares his own foretold return with the coming of a thief in the night (see Matthew 24:43-44). So Boromir's proud refusal to follow the example of his king foreshadows ultimate rejection of Aragorn's authority, and the death to which such hubris leads. It is a marked contrast to the good and humble stewardship of his brother, Faramir.

Man's capacity to betray Christ is not only portrayed in Boromir's tragic moral failure, of course, but also in more mundane day-to-day complicity with evil. When the Hobbits set out from Bree toward Weathertop with Strider as a guide, for example, Bill Ferny has been an active agent in Mordor's plans to thwart their progress. Merry's ponies have been stolen, and Barliman Butterbur takes it upon himself to compensate Merry for the loss. The total? Thirty pieces of silver!

Naturally, the struggle between the faithful and faithless in Tolkien's story is just part of the larger symbolic struggle between light and darkness. The tale of the War of the Ring takes place at the end of the Third Age of Middle-Earth. "The Dark Tower had been rebuilt, it was said," Tolkien writes in an early passage of *The Fellowship of the Ring.* "There were wars and growing fears,"[16] and "rumors of strange things happening in the world outside."[17] This echoes Jesus' instructions about signs of the end of the age: there will be "wars and rumors of wars."[18] Later, in Lórien, the words of the Fellowship's host, Haldir, make explicit the Elvish haven's symbolic nature as a beleaguered beacon in the struggle between "the Shadow" and "the light of the Sun."[19] Lórien is an idyllic paradise, almost existing even outside time, a bulwark against Mordor's darkness and evil, which creeps even on the borders of Lórien from Moria and Mirkwood. In such times, Haldir explains, trust has gone awry.

And still later, in the darkness of Cirith Ungol, Shelob hunts Sam and Frodo, who have been lured there by their faithless guide. As Shelob makes her final charge in the darkness, Sam remembers the Phial of Galadriel, and Frodo draws it from inside his shirt. The light shines forth from the phial, blinding Shelob and sending her scuttling back into the blackness. "The light shines in the darkness, but the darkness has not understood it."[20]

PROVIDENCE AND FREE WILL

Such is the power of darkness in our world, though, that it may prevent us from seeing light, even when light abounds. It's not that the light isn't there; it's just that our hearts are hardened. We have ears that cannot hear, and eyes that cannot see. So it is that readers who ruefully point out the darkness in Tolkien's vision can totally miss the symbolism and spiritual themes which anchor his tale. Taken as a whole, these themes can be used as a powerful witness for the faith of Middle-Earth's creator, and as a tremendous encouragement to the faith of his readers.

The most dominant of these themes is the relationship of *free will* and *providence.* The former is a concept of which we are well aware; and if we are Americans it is best expressed in our constitutional rights to life, liberty and the pursuit of happiness. The latter concept — providence — is one with which we, as humans under modern free-thinking influence, may not be so familiar. In brief, providence affirms "God's faithful and effective care and guidance of everything which He has made toward the end which He has chosen."[21] Providence may often be confused with *fate*, but the two are not the same. Fate overemphasizes causality, and may be contrasted with the answer to the first opening question of the Heidelberg Catechism: "What is your only comfort in life and death?"

> "That I, with body and soul, both in life and in death, am not my own, but belong to my faithful Savior Jesus Christ who... so preserves me that without the will of my Father in heaven not a hair can fall from my head; yea, that all things must work together for my salvation."[22]

Fate says, "It's beyond my control." Providence says, "It's in God's control; and to the extent that I am within God's will, I can be confident in the outcome." Suffering may occur, yes; but we may be sure that there is a purpose behind it — God's purpose, and He's the one who wins all the marbles in the end.

The role of providence is easily discernible in *The Lord of the Rings*. The characters openly discuss it. For instance, while still in the Shire, Gandalf tells Frodo that "Bilbo was *meant* to find the Ring, and *not* by its maker. In which case, you also were *meant* to have it."[23] Frodo is not altogether pleased. "Why was I chosen?" he asks. "You may be sure," Gandalf replies, "that it was not for any merit that others do not possess."[24] Later, on the way to Buckland, Frodo and his friends encounter Elves in the woods. While Sam and the others sleep, Frodo and Gildor talk, and the Elf agrees with Gandalf's assessment. "In this meeting there may be more than chance," he says, "but the purpose is not clear to me."[25]

By the time the Hobbits have arrived at Rivendell, one purpose has become clear: the protection of the Ringbearer and companions from Sauron's Dark Riders. When Frodo has recovered from his wound at Weathertop, Elrond convenes a council to determine a course of action. Not surprisingly, the advice of Elrond is rooted in a sense of providential guidance. "You have come and are here met, in this very nick of time, by chance as it may seem. Yet it is not so," he counsels. "Believe rather that it is so ordered that we, who sit here, and none others, must now find counsel for the peril of the world."[26] Bilbo, the old Hobbit, attempts to introduce a fatalist view, volunteering to carry the Ring to the end of the Quest, seeing as he was the one who seemed to start the whole mess. Elrond overrules, designating Frodo as the Ringbearer. "This task is appointed for you, Frodo,"[27] Elrond says.

So before The Fellowship of the Ring ever departs Imladris, we have a fully developed view of the power of providence: that we may have our own plans for our lives, "but it is the Lord's purpose that prevails";[28] that the divine use of regular folk without special merit demonstrates how divine strength may allow mortal weakness to be overcome; and that as we act to carry out the Lord's purpose through His strength, we demonstrate that we "are God's workmanship, created in Christ Jesus to do good works, which God prepared in advance for us to do."[29]

But providence controls not only the destiny of God's faithful; it controls those straying, and His enemies as well. At the Tombs in the Citadel of Minas Tirith, for instance, Gandalf confronts the despondent and misguided Steward of Gondor, Denethor. "Authority is not given you," Gandalf lectures him, "to order the hour of your death."[30] Similarly, Sauron's wraiths know that their power to wreak evil is limited, and that they must ultimately bow to the Power that guides all things. And they are equally capable of expressing an understanding of providence. The Witch King, for instance, knows enough to declare, "No living man may hinder me!"[31] No, but in his rashness, the wraith speaks these words disdainfully to his most deadly enemies: neither Wizard nor man, but a warrior princess and a Hobbit!

Providence tends to works itself out, as Cowper's hymn famously put it, in "a mysterious way."[32] This is also demonstrated when riders are sent out from Rivendell against the Nine from Mordor: Their assignments are chosen by lot. Glorfindel draws the assignment of chasing off the Ringwraiths guarding the West Road. Within providence, this is not understood as merely drawing straws, but a method of divine guidance, as in the Bible when the disciples need to replace Judas. The Urim and Thummim which guided David and other Hebrew leaders also provided direction from God in much the same way.

Of course, one of the most mysterious ways in which God's providence functions is through free will. And in Tolkien's world, like ours, it's not just the grand and noble who have a part to play in working out the world's destiny. Hobbits, the hunted Wild Men like Ghân-Buri-Ghân, and even women (gasp!) have meaningful and critical roles to play in the War of the Ring. The "'wheels of the world' are often turned," Tolkien wrote, "not by the Lords and Governors, or even gods, but by the seemingly unknown and weak."[33] While these words were intended as private communication to a publisher, they certainly apply to Middle-Earth as well. And if the seemingly unknown and weak are chosen to turn the wheels of the world, the free will they exercise determines much of the way in which God's providence is accomplished. God may "be hungry for mashed potatoes,"[34] as Juan Carlos Ortiz allegorizes, and may be determined to have them; but how the potatoes get planted, harvested, peeled, sliced and cooked (to twist the analogy a bit) depends on the workers, the choices they make, and how long it takes to make them.

One of the choices which surfaces repeatedly in *The Lord of the Rings* is sacrifice, and King Théoden's niece, Éowyn, is on the receiving end of a lecture about it. She longs to be a warrior; but during her uncle's waning years, she is reduced to being the attendant to a seeming dotard. When the King of Rohan is rejuvenated for battle, though, she is left behind as guardian of Théoden's people. She expresses her frustration to Aragorn as he is about to depart on the Paths of the Dead, saying, "May I not now spend my life as I will?" Aragorn responds, "Few may do that with honor."[35] Sacrifice, Aragorn says, is not a one-off concession to necessity, it's a way of life.

Even Jesus struggled with pursuit of his own personal desires, praying in Gethsemane that the fate of the cross might be avoided; and Aragorn expresses the truth of Jesus' decision: that doing the right thing is preferable to pursuing one's own will, no matter how frustrated or underappreciated one may be.

This has been the story of Aragorn's own life: to forego personal desires in favor of a grander, more noble, and prophesied calling; to reclaim the Crown of Gondor. Not only has he spent his already long life as one of the Dúnedain guarding the borders of the Shire, but he has also previously served in the armies of Gondor and Rohan, under the leadership of lesser men. And he has accepted that

Elrond's daughter, Arwen, will only wed him when he sits on the throne of Gondor. Aragorn's focus is never on the present, but always on the future, a future never more in doubt than when he crosses the threshold of the Paths of the Dead.

Before that happens, though, Aragorn also has wise words for Éowyn's brother. Éomer mourns the news of Gandalf's passing; but Aragorn observes, "When the great fall, the less must lead."[36] Aragorn was seasoned enough to have learned one of the 20th century's greatest lessons: that evil will prosper when good men stand by and do nothing. When others begin second-guessing Gandalf's vision, Aragorn asserts that Gandalf's foreknowledge has taken the cost into account. "Do not judge the counsel of Gandalf," he tells Théoden, "until all is over."[37] Count the cost, yes, as Jesus advised his disciples; but act in confidence, and realize that "time is short."[38] And remember that "all we have to decide," as Gandalf puts it, "is what to do with the time that is given us."[39]

Frodo and Sam certainly appreciate that sense of urgency, and the darkness of their likely end. The Fellowship broken, Frodo and his faithful friend continue the mission alone. The weight of the burden finally leads Frodo to subtly observe that to "do this job,"[40] as Sam says, means in all likelihood to die. In sorrow, in sympathy and in pain, Sam takes Frodo's hand and weeps over it. Where does Sam's faithfulness come from? Why is he so willing to follow his friend to likely death in Cirith Ungol? "Greater love has no one than this," Jesus said, "that he lay down his life for his friends."[41]

Sam, of course, never expected to be the one left alone, as he is after Frodo is taken by the Orcs. Convinced for the time being that Frodo is dead, his choices seem few. But in much the same way as he defeated Shelob, somehow he finds the strength to see that he "must not fail."[42] He is driven by a purposeful, sacrificial character: He perseveres. In fact, the "choices of Master Samwise" perfectly demonstrate how "suffering produces perseverance; perseverance, character; and character, hope,"[43] as Paul says in Romans.

And hope does not disappoint Sam: He rescues Frodo, quite improbably. Earlier, as the two struggle up to Cirith Ungol, they speak about the nature of Story — which tales survive and which don't, who has stories told about them and who doesn't. Emphasizing the need to persevere, Sam remarks "We hear about those as just went on."[44] The writer of Hebrews links perseverance directly to faith: Believers "need to persevere so that when you have done the will of God, you will receive what He has promised."[45] And what has God promised? That "those who hope in the Lord will renew their strength. They will soar on wings like eagles; they will run and not grow weary, they will walk and not be faint."[46] Echoing Paul's Old Testament allusion in Romans that the "righteous will live by faith,"[47] Hebrews contrasts "those who shrink back and are destroyed" with "those who believe and are saved."[48] Refusing to shrink back, Frodo and Sam literally soar on the wings of eagles, in the end.

In the same conversation with Sam, Frodo observes that people in stories of perseverance do their deeds and only "go when their part's ended."[49] This is true of all great stories: having "served God's purpose in his own generation," the Apostle Paul observed of King David, he died and "was buried with his fathers."[50]

We all have our own providential part to play, even unredeemable creatures like Gollum. Early on in Tolkien's story, Gandalf comments on Frodo's sensitivity to injustice in the world, particularly with respect to Gollum. "Many that live deserve death. And some that die deserve life. Can you give it to them?"[51] he asks. Providence is at work, of course, even in the case of Gollum; he, too, is part of a grander purpose. In the Emyn Muil, he becomes a guide for Frodo and Sam, a fawning slave; but he is forcibly tamed, and it is only a grudging pretense. In deciding what to do with Gollum, Frodo replays that distant fireside conversation with Gandalf: "Be not too eager to deal out death in the name of justice, fearing for your own safety."[52] And so, with the power of death in his own hand, Frodo relents.

And it is well for Frodo and Sam that they were merciful to Gollum, for the same mercy must be extended to them by Faramir, who finds it necessary to suspend his own law for the sake of the Hobbits. As they have judged others, acting on the knowledge that "mercy triumphs over judgment,"[53] so also they have been judged. Perhaps it is no accident that the only overt religious practice of Middle-Earth is to be found "in 'a glimpse' among Faramir's men"[54] — the Men of Númenor's custom of looking to the west for a moment of silence prior to eating, in honor both of their past and the eternal.

THE PROBLEM OF EVIL

Of course, the ultimate role that Gollum plays is not just as guide for the Hobbits, nor as foil for Faramir's mercy. Providence dictates, rather, that mercy has been necessary for the destruction of the Ring. And so we find that free will and mercy are the bridge between providence and the second great theme in *The Lord of the Rings:* the problem of evil.

Darkness and evil abound in Middle-Earth, of course. And it's not just found in the form of the Dark Lord, Ringwraiths, Orcs and Trolls. The worst kind of evil is that which we find in ourselves: the willingness, for instance, to be deceived. Consider that Théoden's counselor, Gríma, is called "Wormtongue." Whence the nickname? In medieval literature (and likewise in Tolkien's works), *worm* is not the nightcrawler used to bait a fishhook, but a dragon. Not coincidentally, one of the traditional characteristics of dragons is their power to deceive. Even in the Bible, Satan is frequently depicted as the "dragon" or "serpent." He is the Deceiver. At one point, Gandalf rebukes Grima, "Down, snake! Down on your belly!"[55] It is no surprise when he is unmasked as a spy of Saruman: His deceiving tongue is but a poor imitation of his master's voice.

Ironically, Rohan has given Isengard into the keeping of Saruman only to have it become the base of the Orcs' and Wargs' forays against Fangorn and, finally, Rohan. Saruman expected the powers of Isengard to crush Rohan, for he had fortified his position and "made it better, he thought, being deceived."[56] As the deceiver, Satan, is himself deceived and comes to ruin, Saruman learns the same lesson as Simon the Sorcerer in the eighth chapter of Acts: There are some powers that can't be had for any price.

But the power of darkness may still be divisive. When the Fellowship must pass through Lórien in blindfolds, Haldir observes that "In nothing is the power of the Dark Lord more clearly shown than in the estrangement that divides all those who still oppose him."[57] The Fellowship itself is a testimony of the trust possible amongst those of the light; but their blindfolds remind us of the true nature of fellowship: "Whoever loves his brother lives in the light, and there is nothing in him to make him stumble. But whoever hates his brother is in the darkness and walks around in the darkness; he does not know where he is going, because the darkness has blinded him."[58]

The power of Lórien is maintained by the ring that Galadriel wears. But she and Celeborn have other powers as well, including powers of insight. The heart of each member of the Fellowship is searched. For Gimli, "it seemed to him that he looked suddenly into the heart of an enemy and saw there love and understanding."[59] The enmity between the Dwarves and Elves was long-standing and bitter, so the love which Gimli felt was truly a love like that Jesus spoke of when he said, "Love your enemies":[60] a love that "keeps no record of wrongs."[61]

The wedge driven between Dwarves and Elves was designed, naturally, by Sauron's mentor, Morgoth. So it comes as no surprise that loyalties are divided within the band of raiding Orcs which captures Merry and Pippin. Some are loyal to Mordor, while others are loyal to Saruman at Isengard. Deception and division providentially transform the seeming evil of Boromir's betrayal into good; for as Jesus said, "If Satan opposes himself and is divided, he cannot stand; his end has come."[62] The Orcs quarrel amongst themselves, and the delay results in their utter defeat on the borders of Fangorn, delivering Merry and Pippin into the care of Saruman's worst possible foe, Treebeard.

Jesus' warning about division is one which others of the fellowship would do well to take to heart. Many temptations and deceits drive those apart who should be united in a common cause. Even in Lórien, the Ring represents a temptation for Galadriel when Frodo offers to give it to her. She wisely declines, however. "I pass the test," she says, vowing that she "will diminish,"[63] demonstrating much of the same selfless humility as John the Baptist. Why? Because she divines enough of providence to know that there are greater powers at work. "Maybe the paths that you each shall tread are already laid before your feet."[64] Boromir, though, is not the only one who perceives in Galadriel "a choice between a shadow of fear that lay ahead, and something that he greatly desired."[65] But he

does go so far as to openly say, "She was tempting us."[66]
Celeborn and Galadriel know, however, that the only evil
which a man may find in Lórien has been brought by himself. "Each one is tempted," says the Apostle James, "when,
by his own evil desire, he is dragged away and enticed."[67]
By what is Boromir enticed? His own hard-hearted willingness to be divided against his friends. And what is his
evil desire? Power.

Boromir's true colors are revealed on Amon Hen.
His lust for power and glory gets the better of him. "The
fearless, the ruthless — these alone will achieve victory,"[68]
he says to Frodo. Boromir's failure to resist temptation
helps Frodo see the way toward the hard path all the more
clearly; but in that moment of struggle, Frodo is also tempted. In spite of the weight of destiny and providence in
which his task is steeped, Frodo considers, as we have
observed earlier, taking the easy way out. Tolkien tells us
that Frodo was still free to choose his "own way,"[69] and had
the evil of abused power been Frodo's own temptation
things might have gone very differently.

As it did with Saruman. His most powerful tool in
the pursuit of power, the Palantír, turns out to be his undoing. Not only does it expose him to the deceitful malice of
Sauron, it also falls unwittingly (perhaps providentially?)
into the hands of its rightful owner: Aragorn. But don't our
own treasures also turn to our undoing? We can plead ignorance, like Pippin stealing a look into the forbidden globe,
saying, "I had no notion of what I was doing."[70] But all the
while, our conscience tells us otherwise, as Gandalf reminds
Pippin. We simply and willfully choose the wrong course.

When relating some of the history of Númenor to
Frodo and Sam, Faramir draws on the mythology of
Tolkien's "Atalantë," the Fall of Númenor (and, for Tolkien,

the story of "the Second Fall of Man"[71]). Having aided in the defeat of Melkor at the end of the First Age, the Men of Númenor much later return to Middle-Earth to battle the armies of Melkor's lieutenant, Sauron. Temporarily vanquished, Sauron is taken captive to Númenor. Over time, his deceit persuades Ar-Pharazón that men have a right to the Blessed Realm of Valinor; and in their lust for power and deathlessness, the Men of Númenor assault the land of the gods. Númenor's armies are wasted, and their island home disappears beneath the waves of the western ocean. As in Genesis, the lust for immortality leads to the expulsion from paradise. Once again, man has disobeyed God and badly chosen his own path.

A similar confidence in power proves tempting as Aragorn's terrible battle is about to be waged with Mordor. More is at stake than just the loss of life: It seems as if the very fate of Middle-Earth hangs in the balance. In such times, it is only human to place confidence in military strength and wise planning. Gandalf's counsel, however, is that such confidence is misplaced. "Victory cannot be achieved by arms,"[72] he says, echoing the psalmist. And he's not just talking about current events.

So what's the solution for Gandalf, if it isn't armies and military strategy? "It is not our part," he says, "to master all the tides of the world, but to do what is in us for the succor of those years wherein we are set."[73] In other words, success is only found if we are all true to the purpose and work which has been "prepared in advance" for us to do: if we are content to act within providence, rather than take matters into our own hands. Notably, Gandalf speaks not as a man, but as one of the Maiar; and Gondor's destiny hangs not in the balance of fate, but depends on Aragorn's return from the Paths of the Dead, an act very much prepared in advance, and specifically ordained for the returning King.

But man's lust for power has irrevocably shaped the history of Middle-Earth. The power of evil is manifest in a land saturated with the blood of genocide. This doesn't distinguish Middle-Earth; rather, it "gives this imagined world its verisimilitude,"[74] as Tolkien put it. The Third Age is much like the 20th century, and many of the others which have gone before. In fact, genocide figures pretty prominently in the Old Testament, too. This is an appallingly interesting aspect of Tolkien's work, and one that won't be likely to surface in any neo-Disney fantasy.

But again, the hideousness of the slaughter at Helm's Deep, the Pelennor Fields, and even at the Black Gate is precisely what renders Tolkien's theorized "eucatastrophe" meaningful. "We were born in a dark age," as Tolkien said of our own world. "But there is this comfort: otherwise we should not know, or love so much, what we do love."[75] With the victory won, Aragorn may finally claim his bride, having achieved victory even over the Paths of the Dead, and having ascended to his rightful throne. In the same way, Jesus won his bride the Church, only after rising victorious from the grave and ascending to his throne in heaven. And Aragorn's half-Elven bride, Arwen ultimately gives up her own life for her mate, choosing mortality over the immortality of her Elvish kin. In the same way, in becoming the bride of Christ, the Church gives up its life for Him.

Prior to the writing of *The Lord of the Rings*, the theorized tension between "dyscatastrophe" and "eucatastrophe" was, Tolkien wrote, "a mere proposition — which awaited proof."[76] In the vision of Middle-Earth presented in his novel, at least, evil is a "problem" only to the extent that created beings allow themselves to be deceived and divided; succumb to temptation; or are willfully led into blindness by the darkness of this world. "If anguish were visible," Tolkien observed, "almost the whole of this benighted planet would be enveloped in a dense dark vapor."[77] Nonetheless, God is able to turn all seeming evil to his ends, and we must be confident that His long-term view ultimately and finally will bring us the full comfort of salvation.

THE AGE OF MEN

Oddly, though, Tolkien's *dénouement* somewhat defuses his "eucatastrophe." Arguably, the "sudden joyous 'turn'"[78] of deliverance in his story is the destruction of the Ring, the fall of the Dark Tower, and the sweeping arrival of the Eagles at Orodruin. But this "fleeting glimpse" of *evangelium* is tempered by the anticlimactic skirmishes which accompany the Hobbits' return home. And after the Scouring of the Shire, time passes and eventually the weight of having borne the Ring drains both energy *and* joy from Frodo. He joins Bilbo and Gandalf aboard an Elvish ship at the Grey Havens, bound directly for the blessed land in the west to live among the immortal. Joy for Frodo cannot be had in this life; he must pass prematurely into the next to recapture it. Is this eucatastrophe or dyscatastrophe? Perhaps pessimistic eucatastrophe?

The closing chapters of *The Lord of the Rings* are more somber than joyous for many readers. The Scouring of the Shire is not nearly as romantic and grand an escape as the balance of the War of the Ring, even if it is the War's final battle. The rules have changed. "I am with you at present, but soon I shall not be," Gandalf tells the homeward-bound Hobbits while at Bree. "I am not coming to the Shire. You must settle its affairs yourselves; that is what you have been trained for. Do you not yet understand? My time is over: it is no longer my task to set things to rights, nor to help folk do so. And as for you, my dear friends, you will need no help."[79] Bummer.

If there is chaff mixed in Tolkien's corn, this is most likely it: a vision of the future as the mundane Age of Men. In this new Age, the very kinds of dynamic power which yielded Tolkien's potent eucatastrophe are pointedly absent. Contrast Gandalf's words with these: "I am with you a little while longer," said Jesus to his Disciples. "Where I go you cannot follow me now, but you shall follow later. ... He who believes in me, the works that I do, he shall do also; and greater works than these he shall do. ... And I will ask the Father and He will give you another helper... that is, the Spirit of truth. ... In that day you shall know that I am in my Father, and you in me, and I in you."[80]

Chapter Six

TOLKIEN'S "FOURTH AGE"

To this point, our analysis has demonstrated that the writing of *The Lord of the Rings* was motivated by a pure desire to create a story which would honor and glorify the joyous "eucatastrophe" of the gospel. Further, through an examination of the text, we find that the novel is, on the whole, favorably demonstrative of fundamental Christian values and themes. We also know that Tolkien was at least theoretically aware of chaff in his corn. Therefore, it is not patently outrageous to postulate that the vision of the Age of Men which concludes Tolkien's work is problematic.

Problematic, however, does not mean *evil* or *wrong*. As Myth, though, his story attempts to say certain things not only about *evangelium* but about the world in which we live. And as the contrast between Gandalf's words at Bree with those of Jesus suggests, there may be cause to find the things which Tolkien's story says troubling or unsettling. Is our world really one impoverished, one which pales in comparison to Middle-Earth and the dynamic divine power which controls its destiny?

If Tolkien's vision is problematic, there should be evidence external to the text to support such a claim. Before reviewing the evidence, however, it would be well to justify the effort. After all, it is easy to dismiss unease about the closing chapters of *The Lord of the Rings* on grounds that such a subjective reaction falls squarely into the category of anecdotal evidence which Consecration Analysis rejects. After all, a great many readers, if not the majority, are not affected in the same way. We might also rightly point out that if adverse reactions are observed, they are really the results of the reader's own chaff and not Tolkien's.

However, there is hard evidence that Tolkien himself found one or more aspects of his work unsettling. We have already seen that the body of work was influenced by a creative tension between his faith and his rationality. We have also seen that *The Lord of the Rings* was the experimental proving-ground of Tolkien's theory of fairy stories, and first experiments are often imperfectly executed. Further, we have seen that Tolkien's melancholy insistence on the "long defeat" of human existence was in "The Dialog of Finrod and Andreth" moderated by the introduction of true hope. And Tolkien's own son felt that this late tinkering with the mythology was an effort to disarm some "fearful weapon" which his father had created against his own work. What led Christopher to claim that a "potentially destructive doubt had emerged before my father finished work on *The Lord of the Rings*"?[1]

The back-story to *The Hobbit* and *The Lord of the Rings* was written between 1916 and 1937. As Tolkien focused his efforts on his second Hobbit story, the stories of the Elvish mythology went mostly untouched. His most significant efforts in this period were related to experiments with Round World variations on the myths. Then, in 1951, while the details of publishing *The Lord of the Rings* were being worked out, Tolkien undertook extensive revisions to resolve problems of chronology and character histories, and to finally abandon the Round World variations. By 1953, Tolkien told W. H. Auden, the "legendarium" was solidified and complete, consistent with the details of his novels;[2] in particular, the mythology meshed with the details of the Appendices to *The Return of the King* as they would be published in 1955. However, another spate of revision began subsequent to the publication of *The Lord of the Rings*, around 1956, and continued through the mid-60s.

So we find three general (if grossly simplified) phases of mythological development: the Phase One pre-*Rings* development, through 1937; Phase Two refinements driven by issues of consistency and Flat World cosmology, through 1955; and Phase Three post-*Rings* revisions and additions, from 1956 onward. It is in these last two phases, particularly Phase Three, which Christopher Tolkien finds "the record of a prolonged interior debate"[3] resulting from his father's "reinterpretation of central elements in the 'mythology' (or legendarium as he called it) to accord with the imperatives of a greatly modified underlying conception."[4]

What precisely was the nature of this "interior debate"? How was Tolkien's "underlying conception" modified at such a late date in the process, and why? To produce a coherent text for *The Silmarillion* in these later years, Tolkien would need to do much more than merely "decide which version of each chapter he should use,"[5] as Humphrey Carpenter asserts. And while Christopher Tolkien rightly assessed that the debate touched on cosmological issues, he erred, perhaps, in seeing the central issue as the Flat World vs. Round World debate. The evidence suggests another alternative: that, while Phase Two revisions were mostly motivated by temporal issues (time and space: geography, chronology, geology and paleontology) and internal consistency, Phase Three revisions were primarily motivated by theology.

Whatever the reasons for Tolkien's "potentially destructive doubt," it is certain that doubt drove the author to action. And if Tolkien's continued mythological tinkering was motivated by doubt, and not by the mere "habit of drastic rewriting," as Humphrey Carpenter suggests,[6] it follows that we may also be justified in our concern; especially if the source of doubt is to be found in Tolkien's published creation. So a discerning analysis of *The Lord of the Rings* necessarily dissects the issues connected to the author's doubt. If both the author of *The Lord of the Rings* and his son felt there was cause for some concern, there just may be.

Before proceeding with this analysis, though, we shall clarify how Phase Two and Phase Three revisions affect our reading of *The Lord of the Rings*. First, Phase Two revisions were either abandoned or retained. If they were abandoned, they do not affect the Middle-Earth which the reader encounters; if revisions were retained, they have affected in a material way what has been published about Middle-Earth. Not only did these revisions find their way into *The Lord of the Rings* and its extensive Appendices, they also drove the editorial decisions behind the published version of *The Silmarillion*. Phase Two revisions which were retained, then, bring together the entire body of Tolkien's mythology into a cohesive whole, as the author remarked to Auden. Phase Three revisions, however — for good or ill, whether appealing or disturbing — have no effect whatsoever on the content of *The Lord of the Rings*, or how we read it. They can't. What they do provide is an intriguing insight into the working of the author's mind in the wake of critical reaction to his most famous work. If Phase Three revisions helped Tolkien resolve his own doubt, understanding them may also give us some clues as to the proper handling of *The Lord of the Rings*.

MIDDLE-EARTH, TIME AND SPACE

So where in the world *is* the Shire? That's a good question, since Tolkien confessed that Middle-Earth "was devised dramatically rather than geologically or paleontologically. I do sometimes wish," he went on, "that I had made some sort of agreement between the imaginations or theories of the geologists and my map a little more possible."[7] Of course, we have already observed that Tolkien's saga is set somewhere in the northwest of the Old World, and that Tolkien's work was originally intended as a mythology for England.

Not surprisingly, the first concrete geographical reference in Tolkien's notes is, in fact, English. In an early rough story synopsis for a *Hobbit* sequel, Tolkien hurriedly jotted: "Elrond tells [Bilbo] of an island. Britain? Far west where the Elves still reign. Journey to perilous isle."[8] So in Tolkien's mind, the Old World setting of the story was possibly connected to the real, historic England. The maps of Middle-Earth did not yet exist, however, and Tolkien quickly abandoned the island setting for his sequel. (While the "perilous" island does not explicitly figure into *The Lord of the Rings*, we shall see presently that the influence of this early conception persisted.) As the story of the War of the Ring developed and the historical connections to the background mythology became more pronounced, geographical ties to England grew more evident.

"If Hobbiton and Rivendell are taken (as intended) to be at about the latitude of Oxford," Tolkien remarked in reference to the scale of the setting for the story, "then Minas Tirith, 600 miles south, is at about the latitude of Florence. The mouths of Anduin and the ancient city of Pelargir are at about the latitude of ancient Troy."[9] Note, though, that Tolkien did not argue for a "true" geographic correlation; he merely fixed the place-names of Middle-Earth upon the known map of Europe.

From a literary standpoint, this shouldn't present particularly perplexing difficulties. Tolkien designed a truly mythic story, ostensibly grounded in history, not *actually* grounded in history. Hence, his characters are free to travel great distances in flat, two-dimensional space. Their movements make perfect sense on the maps published with the books. This two-dimensionality, however, is part of the Flat World problem Tolkien mentioned in his letters: a dramatic locale free of the cartographic problems of the earth's curvature. Fortunately, in Flat World myths, there's really no need for geographic consistency.

Even in historic accounts written by those with some knowledge of modern astronomy, geography is difficult to make sensible. The New World maps and travelogues recorded by the Spanish explorer Cabeza de Vaca are a perfect example. There is no doubt that he and his companions really did wander for years along the Gulf coast and across New Spain, but the lands he describes defy correlation with known historic locations. Early explorers' maps of the African continent are equally puzzling. And if we can't really make heads or tails of the detailed movements of the Hebrews in the biblical wilderness, why would we demand more from a fictional history? Is the sketchy detail of Thror's map any problem in appreciating *The Hobbit*? No; and Tolkien's sequel takes place in the same distant past, when mapmaking techniques could not have been far advanced.

Which raises a more thorny question: When, exactly, in our past did Tolkien's story supposedly take place? Subjective impressions vary widely. If one pays attention to waistcoats, pipeweed, buttons and leather-bound books, one might fix the War of the Ring within the not-too-distant past; if one pays attention to geologic discontinuities and more metaphysical considerations, one can easily postulate a pre-historic setting. If one pays attention to both, one mostly gets confused. "Though I have not attempted to relate the shape of the mountains and the land masses to what geologists may say or surmise about the nearer past," Tolkien clarifies obscurely, "imaginatively this 'history' is supposed to take place in a period of the actual Old World of this planet."[10] Big help, that. At least Tolkien clarifies that the problems of "land masses" are in essence literary, not physical, and do not require postulation of the passing of geologic epochs. The lands suit the needs of the story, not the needs of modern geographers.

But Tolkien does provide three fairly specific historic reference points. The first of these is the Creation. Okay, not much real help there, unless one accepts Archbishop James Ussher's attempt in 1650 to establish the exact date that the world was created, based on a literal interpretation of biblical chronologies. (The Latter Day Saints, among other faiths, still use Ussher's timetable as a definitive reference.) Rather than proceed from creation as a starting point, however, we will focus instead on the second of Tolkien's anchor points: the drowning of Atlantis.

Of course, Atlantis is not a historic reference point at all, in the conventional sense. But we are not dealing with actual history; in myth we are dealing with ostensible history, such as that of Atlantis. In Plato's account, written around 350 B.C., the drowning of Atlantis is already an event of the distant past. Scholars generally agree that Plato's timing for the supposed event would place it at about 9000 B.C.

Within the history of Middle-Earth, this anchor point is roughly the end of the Second Age, the Downfall of Númenor. Tolkien stated many times that he had a long-standing Atlantis obsession, manifested in dreams and nightmares of a gigantic wave. He once remarked that an early attempt at a time-travel story to Atlantis (suggested by C. S. Lewis) was an attempt to purge the obsession.[11] Originating as an idea outside his mythology, the locale of the story was gradually transferred to the T-mythical Númenor; and when an obsession with Númenor overtook the artificial time-travel impetus for the story, the "accidental" Númenor-Atlantis connection was absorbed into his mythology. It was formally and completely integrated (apparently) during Phase Two revisions, specifically the period from 1951-1955 when details of the lineage of Elrond and Isildur needed to be worked out.

The story of "the great 'Atlantis' isle of Númenórë" is also tied to the Biblical deluge, according to Tolkien. "Elendil, a Noachian figure," he wrote, "is borne high upon the towering waves that bring ruin to the West of Middle-Earth. He and his folk are cast away as exiles upon the shores."[12] We have discussed earlier how the deceit of Sauron corrupted Ar-Pharazón, who proudly provoked the Valar into destruction of Númenor. And in "a kind of Noachian situation the small party of the Faithful"[13] find their way to Middle-Earth. So for Tolkien, the biblical deluge is the same event as the drowning of Atlantis; and this is also the same event as the Fall of Númenor in the T-mythology.

To fix dates for the events of Middle-Earth, then, we need only attach a date to the "uber-mythic" deluge and calibrate accordingly. This approach yields a broad range of possibilities. At one extreme would be the date proposed by Greek myth — 9000 B.C. — and at the other would be Ussher's conservative date, roughly 2300 B.C. If one modifies Ussher's approach with a non-literal interpretation of the patriarchal period, one may arrive at an alternate date around 5000 B.C.. These dates, then, somewhere between 9000 and 2300 B.C., roughly correlate to the end of the Second Age of Middle-Earth.

With the end of the Third Age placed 3163 years after the Downfall of Númenor, Ussher's timing becomes difficult to reconcile since the Third Age would end roughly at 860 A.D. When we throw into the mix Tolkien's assertion that "the gap in time between the Fall of Barad-dûr" and modern times is "about 6000 years,"[14] we can see that there's not much point in sticking to Ussher's estimates, as far as Middle-Earth is concerned. Instead, the Platonic or non-literal patriarchy dating systems are a better fit, ranging from somewhere between 6000 and 2000 B.C. Tolkien's estimate falls squarely in between.

The Third Age, then, is decidedly post-diluvian, and we may envision the exploits of the biblical patriarchs simultaneously taking place in Far Harad and the vicinity. The Age of Men, the Fourth Age, dawns while the Incarnation is yet a distant future event, destined to take place in a remote corner of Middle-Earth. Even allowing generously for slop in these estimates, the Fourth Age would be truly pagan, pre-Christian, pre-Roman and even pre-Greek.

Our third anchor point is much more concrete, and brings Tolkien's mythology into the historic period. A central character of Tolkien's original Atlantis time-travel story is a figure co-opted from actual history: Prince "Aelfwine of England (c. 900 AD), called by the Elves Eriol, who being blown west from Ireland eventually came upon the 'straight road' and found Tol Eressëa the Lonely Isle,"[15] as Tolkien later mythologized. After Tolkien abandoned the time-travel tale, his "perilous isle" became Tol Eressëa. This Elvish land lay west of the Enchanted Islands which the Valar set in the Great Sea to bar men forever from Valinor. In Tol Eressëa, Aelfwine encounters the Elvish bard Pengolod, who recounts to him the tale of Númenor along with the body of Elvish history. As late as 1960, Tolkien continued to explicitly "feign" (as he described it to Mrs. Farrar in 1948[16]) that his tales were translated from those obtained by Aelfwine from Pengolod, in both oral and written form.

The feigned source materials for *The Silmarillion*

and related Elvish myths was one of the stickier wickets connected to the Round World Phase Two revisions. "The Elvish myths are 'Flat World,'" Tolkien told Mrs. Farrar. "A pity really but it is too integral to change it."[17]   So the Round World attempts were ultimately abandoned, and the straight road to Tol Eressëa remains the sole link between the Flat World myths and our very real round world.

The latter day copies of the "Red Book of Westmarch," however, are not clearly connected to Aelfwine. So the feigned "discovery" of the account of the War of the Ring is dependent on historic preservation of a physical manuscript. Its "translation" must be explained apart from Aelfwine and Pengolod because copies of the Red Book were not preserved by Elvish bards in Tol Eressëa through the long ages. Tolkien's source materials must have been otherwise protected and preserved in Northwestern Europe.

That a large, leather-bound book might have existed in 4000 B.C. is in itself improbable; but that it might survive into the modern era would be unprecedented. Other technological difficulties also present themselves — umbrellas, tomatoes, clocks, the aforementioned waistcoats, pipeweed and buttons; and, more significantly, explosives. China may have stolen its secrets from Dale, or from other Wizards that ventured into the East; but the kind of explosion which bursts the culvert at Helm's Deep was not Magic, being the work of Orcs. It's the product of the same kind of perverted, corrupt technology that rebuilds Sandyman's mill. Many millennia will pass before this kind of technology actually surfaces in historical accounts.

Tolkien was aware of these anachronisms, of course, and made significant attempts during Phase Two revisions to diminish the scale of the problem. What may nag some readers about the visible remaining elements is how closely

Middle-Earth's technology resembles that which emerged in the period of Tolkien's own philological specialty. The technology is uniquely Medieval Western European, not ancient Sumerian, Egyptian, Greek, Roman or Chinese. So there is no easy answer to be had about the real-world connection between the end of the Third Age of Middle-Earth and actual historical chronologies.

We can be confident, though, that many ages pass between Frodo's day and our own. And we can be confident that the tale recorded is completely pre-Christian, being the "story of what happened B.C. in year X,"[18] as Tolkien put it in 1956. And in the intervening ages, nothing happens to make Christ's appearance in the story anything more than symbolic. Even in what little remains in Tolkien's writing about Aelfwine's visit to Tol Eressëa in 900 A.D., there is no indication that Pengolod had made any connection between the Elvish myths and the true *evangelium*. Should he?

Not at all. If we chronologically equate Tolkien's First through Fourth ages with the period predating Christ, this would allow us to "imagine," as Tolkien did, that we are now "actually at the end of the Sixth age, or in the Seventh."[19] Pengolod and the Elves of Tol Eressëa, then, have been long dissociated from the affairs of men. Their ages-long absence from Middle-Earth wholly justifies ignorance of the Incarnation, especially considering that the T-mythology is told from an Elvish perspective. *The Lord of the Rings* itself, "originating" in documents written thousands of years before Christ, is also necessarily ignorant of the Incarnation.

So the T-mythology is couched in terms which one may call *Judeo-Christian* if by that term one really means *patriarchal-monotheistic*. This is perhaps not alarming; but it does put Tolkien's mythology more in a class with

Judaism or Zoroastrianism than Christianity; and it points us toward a frank admission that Christian symbolism does not yield a Christian world view. If it did, the United States, among other Western countries, would be truly Christian. The 2000 years dominated by the symbol of the cross would have progressed differently than they have.

Middle-Earth is no different. Tolkien is realist enough to understand how symbolism may stand against darkness; but Middle-Earth is also a broken world, and functions like one. The New Testament is clear in demonstrating that a pre-Christological world view is one which makes accepting the person of Jesus as the Christ extremely difficult. So the Messiah would likely be no more welcome in Gondor than He was in Jerusalem; which is well, since Tolkien had no intention of writing the Incarnation into his story. Aelfwine's failure to connect Christianity with Pengolod's stories, however, is a little odd, given that he lived in a Christianized era. His mind seems to be a completely open, blank book.

Perhaps unfortunately, the average reader of *The Lord of the Rings* is completely ignorant of the complex issues discussed above. The more interested fan may glean much of the history of the First through Third Ages from the Appendices in *The Return of the King*. None but the most aggressive, however, will delve so deeply as to have a well-formulated idea of the time-space framework of Middle-Earth. So when it comes to Tolkien's Fourth Age, the Age of Men, readers are mostly left to judge for themselves what age was intended. And many visualizations, including Peter Jackson's filmed adaptation, bear a strong resemblance to Medieval England.

Tolkien's readers may be confused by the supposed timing of Tolkien's tale, some, as I did for a long time, seeing it as contemporary with Arthurian legend or Beowulf, others reading it as ante-diluvian. But such difficulties did not drive Tolkien's "prolonged interior debate," and the consequent mythological revisions. Tolkien, in fact, dismissed these less weighty concerns on various grounds.

First, he pointed out that perception counts a great deal in the matter. Different readers' reactions may vary widely. On the one hand, he observed, "some people find the anachronisms amusing,"[20] while others, seeking unreasonably concrete "explanations in such a world," may find themselves wrapped up in overly-complex and "unneeded reflections."[21] Second, he explained the anachronisms as being the by-product of a necessarily difficult and inaccurate process of translation, tolerable "only as a deliberate 'Anglicization'" to contrast the Hobbits with "other peoples in the most familiar terms."[22] Finally, he appealed to the inner consistency of his created world: If one were to point out to Elves that our world is not like theirs, "the Elves would claim 'Well, that is another Tale. It is not our Tale.'"[23] They might even claim, as Tolkien did, that it is "probably to Sauron that we may look for a solution of the problem of chronology."[24] One can't expect complete consistency from any broken world.

But the most remarkable development in Tolkien's Phase Three revisions is nonetheless related to the long years between the Fall of Barad-dûr and Aelfwine's visit to Tol Eressëa. And it is also related to the curious, unrecorded events happening in the Far East of Middle-Earth during those very dark ages.

FAITH IN TOLKIEN'S FOURTH AGE

The unexpected success of *The Lord of the Rings* naturally led its publishers to request a sequel from Tolkien. But there was a good reason why one was never written — Tolkien couldn't bring himself to write it. He did begin a story called *The New Shadow*, "placed about 100 years after the Downfall [of Mordor], but it proved both sinister and depressing."[25]   While the Hobbits are busy replanting and rebuilding the Shire, and "Aragorn far away on the throne of Gondor" reforges ancient alliances and labors "to preserve some memory"[26] of ages past, the spiritual state of Middle-Earth in the Fourth Age remains bleak. "It is a monotheistic world of 'natural theology,'" Tolkien wrote, and not as an endorsement. "The Third Age was not a Christian world,"[27] he clarified; and the Fall of Barad-dûr did nothing to change that.

If anything, the Fourth Age grows darker. Sauron has been thrown down, yes, and his armies are destroyed, dismantled, or dispersed. But the Fourth Age is also marked by the departure of the Elves. The boat upon which Frodo and Bilbo embark from the Grey Havens is only one of many, and as the Elves depart from Middle-Earth so also fades the effects of their influence. The Magic of Imladris and Lothlórien dies, and is gone forever. Likewise, Tolkien's introduction to *The Lord of the Rings* makes it pretty plain that the time of the Hobbits is nearing an end as well. No more stories about them would be forthcoming in the Fourth Age. So, like the Elves, Hobbits pass out of God's providence in working out the fate of man in the Fourth Age and beyond.

Man is alone in the Fourth Age. In whatever trials may come, Wizards will not provide counsel or aid. Whatever Elves remain are so diminished in power as to be invisible or nearly so, not to mention completely disinterested in the affairs of men. There will be no Hobbits to rise up in unexpected, unlooked-for heroism. And if Gandalf's assertion that "victory cannot be achieved by arms" is to be taken as a general truism, how does a resident of Middle-Earth in the Fourth Age — a person of faith — deal with the growing darkness? A profile of the Fourth Age Believer is illuminating.

First, the Fourth Age Believer believes there is a God. He is called Eru, or Ilúvatar. He is the Creator, and is in charge of all things. He has a plan, and His providence takes all things into account. He also has the latitude to work in strange and mysterious ways, and is not account-able even to the Valar's understanding of Him, much less man's. So far, so good.

Second, the Fourth Age Believer understands that there are lesser gods, the Ainur: the Valar and the Maiar. Once active in the shaping and affairs of the world, they have now, with the departure of the Wizards, wholly removed themselves. In the mode of what we might call *guardian angels*, they appeared even in the Third Age, and helped guide great struggles against incarnated Evil, as was seen in the War of the Ring. But with the Passing of the Ring, such direct assistance can no longer be expected. In fact, the last known "angel" — Gandalf — explicitly said that such aid was no longer forthcoming.

Third, the Fourth Age Believer understands that this is the "Age of Men." This is explicit. It is accepted as fact. The Elves have either passed into the west, or will eventu-ally fade until they become just a memory. And yet, this is not the age of men's glory; that was in the past, the glory of the Númenoreans. Some of that glory still exists in the per-son of King Aragorn; but he is an exception, a mere reminder of the glory of the past, not a promise of the glory of the future. Aragorn is truly long-lived. But that is a spe-cial dispensation, and his seed will soon diminish to a more ordinary lifespan. Man is the chosen race of the age, yes; but men are less than they were, and will become less yet in the near future.

Fourth, the Fourth Age Believer's understanding of

death is less than clear, and it is fearful. The loremasters know that Eru intended death as a strange "gift" to men; but most folk don't see it that way. And the only other clue is a promise of the "remaking of Arda," in which all things will be set right. But this doesn't help much in the present: it is not at all clear how the promise of a future cleansing of evil from the world helps deal with the broken, fallen world of which man is a part and in which man must live.

And so, from day to day, the Fourth Age Believer lives knowing that the Race of Man is diminished; that man is fallen in a fallen world; that there is still evil in the world, and that it is up to man, and man alone, a fallen race, to deal with it; and that the fear of aging and death is ever-present. Even the Fourth Age's first King, Aragorn himself, will abdicate the will to live rather than end his life in infirmity. Gandalf will not come back from the dead to lead men to victory; Tom Bombadil cannot be expected to rescue man from Barrow Wights; men's lips will not produce ecstatic utterances under Elvish influence so that the power of Elbereth may be summoned in aid. Man is left with a mystery, and vague promises; no Savior, no Advocate, no Comforter, no guardian angels, and no promise of such; "no certainty and no knowledge, only fears, or dreams in the dark."[28] Man has only his own bootstraps with which to pull himself up, and faith that God is in control. And the righteous shall have no choice but to live by that faith.

Okay. Now, this is not an impossible state, theologically. Abraham was reckoned righteous, after all, because he lived by faith, so he was no better off than our Fourth Age Believer. Or was he? Let's see... Abraham did have visits from angels; he did have a miracle baby; he did have a ram in the thicket. Arguably, though, these were later blessings for his prior faithfulness, the results of a life-long spiritual journey without such explicit assurances and miraculous events. Abraham drew near to God, so to speak, so God drew nearer to him.

But the spiritual state of our Fourth Age Believer, or even that of Abraham in Ur, is essentially the state of the unsaved in our modern world — the state of those who wish to be faithful to what *has* been revealed to them of God, no matter how little, *in the absence of the gospel.* To the theologically generous, modern pagans simply find themselves in the same boat as our Fourth Age Believer: Have they been faithful? To the theologically restrictive, however, such pagans (and our Fourth Age Believer) are damned.

So Tolkien's Fourth Age is a pagan Fourth Age. We have seen that Tolkien's first mythological urge was escapist. Then, "once upon a time," he told Milton Waldman in 1951, he "had a mind to make a more or less connected body of legend" which he could dedicate to England.[29] This is the motive which drove Phase One development of the T-mythology. At some point during this development, he formulated the thesis of "On Fairy Stories," which would be tested in the writing of *The Lord of the Rings.*

Tolkien's desire for a uniquely English mythology was not entirely supplanted, however, by his later aims for an "eucatastrophic" homage. Humphrey Carpenter misleadingly points out that Tolkien called his original desire "absurd" in his lengthy letter to publisher Milton Waldman in 1951, and suggests that Tolkien later disparaged the desire.[30] Tolkien's letter to Mr. Waldman, however, does not represent a change in Tolkien's thinking. In 1937, when writing to Stanley Unwin — also a publisher — he was able to refer to his mythology as "beloved nonsense," yet still champion it as "elaborate and consistent."[31] Tolkien's letter to Mr. Waldman may call the original aim "absurd"; but this is merely the way Tolkien self-deprecatingly referred to his work when communicating with publishers. It's the self-conscious language of an author aware of a publisher's critical eye.

And in the letter to Mr. Waldman, written while completing the Phase Two revisions of the T-mythology, Tolkien could still assert that his story must not contain "the Christian religion." This was the flaw, he felt, of Arthurian legend. "It is involved in, and explicitly contains the Christian religion. For reasons which I will not elaborate, that seems to me fatal."[32] If anything, Tolkien's letter to Mr. Waldman represents a continuity of thought and purpose, not a changing of course.

We may then be confident — because Tolkien was confident — that we will not find Christianity in *The Lord of the Rings*, nor in the Phase Two T-mythology. We may be confident that this is so due its fundamental, original design, and may also be confident that the faith of the Fourth Age Believer is not a Christian faith.

The chances of a Fourth Age Believer being justified before God are, at best, as slim as the chances in Abraham's day, if not slimmer. The Bible is not terribly complementary about man's ability to be faithful to God in the pre-Mosaic period, or any pagan era. And our portrait of the Fourth Age Believer is generous; our Fourth Age Believer is one of the enlightened, with some knowledge of the Eldar and the Faithful of Númenor, and what that really meant. The vast majority of the people of Middle-Earth are in an even greater darkness than our Fourth Age Believer.

The divine economy in the Fourth Age is depressed, and grace is limited. The only vestiges of truly Christian thought can be symbols or types, which are great. But the Old Testament is packed with symbols, types and explicit prophecies which require the lens of the New Testament to be properly viewed and interpreted. Without the New Testament, the Old Testament is not Christian at all, it's

Jewish *Tanakh*. Jews today are entirely content that their reverence for *Tanakh* does not make them Christian.

The most unsettling aspect of Tolkien's fiction is not its depiction of Magic and Wizards; it's not a gruesome depiction of evil, nor good's violent resistance; it's not even the general darkness of Middle-Earth and the Fourth Age; nor is it, as Christopher Tolkien felt, cosmological inconsistencies. It's this: If the reader is a contemporary counterpart to our Fourth Age Believer — has never heard the gospel, is completely unaware of the nature of Tolkien's faith and has no human guide to Christ — the reader may experience eucatastrophic joy and still, like the Fourth Age Believer, have no real hope for the future. Simply put, one who does not know Christ will not find Him in *The Lord of the Rings* without some external help.

Of course, there's no reason to levy such expectations on *The Lord of the Rings*, or any other fiction. We are aware that it's not the gospel, and it doesn't need to be, allegorically or otherwise. But our expectations are not the issue: Tolkien's expectations are. And one of his own expectations was that his story should point to the *evangelium*. Tolkien was not at all content with the merely happy ending: His goal was a glimpse of the genuine joy of the one true mythic eucatastrophe, that of the resurrection. The evidence suggests that he was disappointed to find that *The Lord of the Rings* had not succeeded to the extent he had wished. Many readers catch a glimpse, yes; but they are as often likely to interpret this glimpse as a look into the glory of England's pagan past.

FOURTH AGE QUESTIONS, FIRST AGE ANSWERS

Both the attentive reader and the defensive Tolkien fan will have noticed that the discussion of our Fourth Age Believer, thus far, has entirely neglected the messianic prophecy found in "The Dialog of Finrod and Andreth." Just so, and for good reason. We have addressed the Fourth Age Believer only in the context of *The Lord of the Rings;* that is, only in the context of Tolkien's Phase One and Phase Two mythological developments. Why? Because Phase Three developments do not, and cannot, affect how the first-time or casual reader understands *The Lord of the Rings.*

So let's pose an interesting question: Were the Dialog to be published as an Appendix to *The Lord of the Rings*, what effect would that have on the reader? How would it modify our understanding of the Fourth Age Believer? Before suggesting answers, let's review the setting, purpose and content of the Dialog.

Finrod is an Elvish King of the First Age, and Andreth is a human woman. Finrod has dwelt with the Valar in Valinor and was alive before the dawn of men. Andreth is one of the Wise, a loremaster. Many generations have passed since her people came out of the east and joined with the exiled Elves in war against Morgoth. Andreth enjoys a special relationship with Finrod, and the two often seek each other for counsel and even personal discourse. Each respects the other immensely.

But because they are of different races, and of wildly differing lifespans, there are fundamental differences between them. There are a host of things that they just don't understand about each other. In particular, their perspective on providence is quite different. The Elves, having dwelt and spoken directly with the Valar and having taken counsel from them, are supremely confident of their place in the cosmos. They may not know the detail of the Music of the Ainur because they did not share in it, but they have full confidence that Eru is in control, and that the Valar will work to secure the fore-ordained destiny of the Elves. However, Elves often become weary of the long struggle.

After a millennium or two, the tension between passion for Middle-Earth's living things and efforts to preserve the world from Morgoth's destructive powers becomes oppressive.

On the other hand, men have been broken almost from their beginning. They even know that they are of a different substance from the Elves, who are a people of dualistic nature: beings with an eternal spirit housed in a perishable, impermanent body. Men, on the other hand, were never meant to physically perish: Their bodies and souls were intended to be permanently one, fused for eternity. In days which men have forgotten, and would not discuss even if they remembered, Morgoth corrupted that design. Men, in their own folly, believed and followed his lies. They have never communed with the Valar, and their lifespan is so short as to make daily survival of higher priority than metaphysical speculation.

These issues form the basis of the Dialog. Why, Finrod wants to know, do men fear physical death? For Elves, the death of the body, possible only through grave injury or loss of the will to live, is no cause for grief. It is a release of the spirit to dwell in the Halls of Mandos until Arda should be remade. Separation from the physical body is not sorrowful. The body is an impermanent housing.

For men, however, loss of the physical body is not the same. Andreth explains that death is a partial loss of intended Being; and what happens to a man's spirit after death is uncertain. Men's spirits do not dwell permanently with Mandos; and a remade Arda offers no hope, as the role of man seems unrelated to the remaking. Man was intended by Eru to find fulfillment in the present world, and that design has been forever marred.

As noted previously, Finrod then presses Andreth

about the question of faith: do not men share in *estel*, the confident hope of the Elves? Andreth points out that *estel* seems based in "certainty" and "knowledge," of which men have none: just "dreams in the dark. But hope? Hope, that is another matter, of which even the Wise seldom speak."[33] Very surprised, Finrod gains this profound insight into the character of men: they are so melancholy, so given to living their lives in furious, destructive passion or quiet desperation because they do not have the confidence of an Elvish faith. They have only a vague, ill- defined prophecy of a future redeemer. Hope unrealized is not the same as confident faith, and man's destiny is dark without a savior.

So how does the Dialog affect the faith of our Fourth Age Believer? It introduces prophecy, but it is a prophecy only known to the Wise, and not discussed openly among them. It looks forward to the future, yes; but only from a Christian perspective could it be interpreted as Christological. Today we can see that the Age of Men led directly to the Incarnation of Jesus of Nazareth. True hope is indeed in man, One man in particular.

For the pagan Fourth Age Believer, however, the Dialog cannot lead to saving faith. The Dialog does not materially improve the Fourth Age Believer's spiritual state. Why, then, should Finrod's insight into the nature of man be so important to us? Because it was important to Tolkien.

The Dialog, according to Christopher Tolkien's analysis in *Morgoth's Ring*, could not have originated any earlier than 1959,[34] and was likely completed later. Uncharacteristic of Phase Three revisions, the Dialog was not only fully realized, it was typed in a clear manuscript instead of Tolkien's usual combination of drafts with hand-written notes. Further, it was accompanied by a detailed commentary, almost as long as the Dialog itself; and it served as a foundational reference for other Phase Three writings. The Dialog is a late work with which Tolkien took utmost care, one to which he attached great importance. It appears, in fact, to be the only wholly original tale which Tolkien completed in the years following his retirement in 1959.

Christopher theorized that the purpose was to "fully explore for the first time the nature of 'the Marring of Men.'"[35] Yes, but not that only. If Tolkien wanted to demonstrate, as he said in his commentary on the Dialog, that death "is 'natural' to men,"[36] he also wanted to demonstrate that man's attitude about death would remain fatalistic until man should understand the need for a redeemer. All people need the same insight into their state which Finrod gains.

The Dialog is "not presented as an argument of any cogency for Men in their present situation (or the one in which they believe themselves to be)," Tolkien explained, "though it may have some interest for Men who start with similar beliefs or assumptions to those held by the Elvish king Finrod."[37] This is a dense statement, which warrants close examination. Who are those whose beliefs are similar to Finrod's? And who are those for whom the Dialog will not be a cogent argument?

Neither group are residents of Tolkien's fictional world. The commentary on the Dialog is not feigned to be written by anyone but Tolkien himself, and its audience is the present day reader of his First Age Dialog. So who, among present day readers, have beliefs like Finrod's? We don't have any Elves with dual natures amongst us, do we? No, we don't have any Elves. But many people do have dualistic faiths of various varieties; and a great many people, like Finrod, have an imperfect understanding of man's true nature: of God's perfect intent in our design; of the Evil One's role in tempting man to forsake it; of man's fundamental fallenness in rejecting God's design and willfully embracing a deception; of the futility of a life without the hope of salvation. Many of Tolkien's readers are, like Finrod at the beginning of the Dialog, unaware of Christianity's claims about the nature of man. They are also unaware of the promise of hope Andreth shares in the Dialog, and they are most certainly living without saving knowledge — that Andreth's hope has been realized in the person of Jesus, the Christ.

Tolkien may therefore be interpreted as saying, "The Dialog is not presented as a cogent argument for those who correctly understand their relationship to their Maker (or even those who falsely think they do), but it may prove enlightening to those who find they *don't* understand the fallenness of man, or how it may be righted." The Dialog is both mythic apologetics, and a tool for evangelism.

This conclusion is perhaps startling considering, as we have already seen, that Tolkien stated during the writing of *The Lord of the Rings* that the appearance of "the Christian religion" in his myth would be "fatal." Unfortunately, Tolkien never fully explained this statement. But as late as 1965, Tolkien was able to clarify that he didn't "feel under any obligation to make my story fit with formalized Christian theology." He goes on, though, to say of *The Lord of the Rings:* "I actually intended it to be consonant with Christian thought and belief."[38]

Tolkien, then, saw that "fitting with formalized theology" was not at all the same thing as being "consonant with thought and belief." The former would require, for instance, that the theology of Middle-Earth conform to the doctrine of the Trinity. The latter has no such stringent requirements, though it does demand that his work not deny specifically Christian beliefs.

Tolkien, the noted philologist, master of languages

and their use, a man well-equipped to say precisely what he intended, chose his words deliberately. He did not tell W. H. Auden that "*The Lord of the Rings* IS consonant with Christian thought and belief." Significantly, he told Auden that it was "actually *intended* to be." Our analysis has shown this intent; but it has also shown that, properly speaking, the intent was not perfectly fulfilled: Christian thought and belief is empty without Christ. And by 1965, particularly after having completed the Dialog, Tolkien himself could see that this was so.

If the Dialog was so important, however, why did Tolkien never pursue its publication? *The Hobbit*, after all, was substantially revised in the 1951 edition, entirely changing the terms of Bilbo's riddle game with Gollum,[39] in order to make it consistent with the tale as it is told in *The Lord of the Rings*. Couldn't the Dialog have been added to the Appendices in *The Return of the King*?

This is a question to which we will never have an answer. It's possible that Tolkien felt, like Flannery O'Connor, that failing to let go of his subcreation would be an attempt to interfere with God's task: For better or worse, he must let God deal with people's hearts through what the art already was. Still, to Christopher Tolkien it seemed that the Phase Three writings were part of a "massive upheaval" that was never completed. From that perspective, Tolkien's later work may have been an attempt, very late in the game, to "revise the tales to make them mesh with Christian theology,"[40] as Regina Doman puts it; but one which never found its way into any easily digestible, published form. And as the vast majority of Tolkien's readers never even make it through *The Silmarillion* (much less *Unfinished Tales* or any of the 12 volumes of the *History of Middle-Earth*) the world that the reader finds is not Tolkien's revised world, but the problematic one which he himself saw the need to address. Truly, as Tolkien began *The Lord of the Rings*, he "had little idea where he was going: it was a beginning without a destination."[41]

HANDLING THE FEARFUL WEAPON

Still, no sin or great fault has been committed by Tolkien. As we have already noted, he had attempted a work which might "rekindle an old light in the world" and "testify for God and Truth,"[42] all the while realizing that a "writer may be basically 'benevolent'" in intent "and yet not be 'beneficent' owing to error and stupidity."[43] Especially in view of the Dialog, it would be gracious to acknowledge that Tolkien's work is both benevolent and beneficent, if humanly (and naturally) imperfect. The Dialog, in particular, may be a powerful tool; and the issue is, rather like the handgun or the knife on our kitchen counter, not whether Tolkien's work can be harmfully misused but whether we let it be. Ultimately, the responsibility lies not with Tolkien, but with his readers.

And we are not only responsible for ourselves. Our evangelical imperative dictates that we are also watchmen put in charge of others. As God explained to Ezekiel,

> "Hear the word I speak and give them warning from me. When I say to a wicked man, 'You will surely die,' and you do not warn him or speak out to dissuade him from his evil ways in order to save his life, that wicked man will die for his sin, and I will hold you accountable for his blood. But if you do warn the wicked man and he does not turn from his wickedness or from his evil ways, he will die for his sin; but you will have saved yourself. Again, when a righteous man turns from his righteousness and does evil, and I put a stumbling block before him, he will die. Since you did not warn him, he will die for his sin. The righteous things he did will not be

remembered, and I will hold you accountable for his blood. But if you do warn the righteous man not to sin and he does not sin, he will surely live because he took warning, and you will have saved yourself."[44]

As ambassadors for Christ, we have been entrusted with the story of the True Eucatastrophe of the Gospel; and one of the worst possible uses of "the time that has been given us," as Gandalf puts it, would be to sit back and take potshots at artists like Tolkien who have been as true to their Savior as they know how.

A Christian Tolkien fan who is aware of the Dialog of Finrod and Andreth may be, in fact, in the position God explained to Ezekiel. We possess knowledge about Tolkien's art — apologetic in form, and useful as pre-evangelism — which would be tragic if left unused.

Perhaps by coming to this realization, we can be what Tarkington described as the best possible audience: "one that will be fair enough to suspend judgment until it has first found out what [the artist] is trying to do; then is competent enough to discover how well he does it; and finally is so all-wise as to know whether or not it's worth doing."[45]

Chapter Seven

COMPELLING ALTERNATIVE VIEWS

Of the hundreds of messages I have received at Hollywood Jesus over the last several years, one of my favorites was the shortest. The exchange went as follows:

To Greg: You are a long-winded fool.

Response: There is certainly that possibility. Thanks for expressing the thought so efficiently; others have needed many more words.... — Greg

I humbly admit that a great number of readers have found my conclusions about Tolkien's fiction absurd. In part, this is due to the extremely difficult task of communicating complex ideas piecemeal, on web pages, over the course of better than two years. It's also due to the fact that I'm not perfect, and have made a number of human errors, both in facts and in presentation. And I would be remiss in failing to note that my thinking about Tolkien has benefited greatly from the extensive dialog at Hollywood Jesus.

So I must also humbly admit that my own warped lens is not the only one through which Tolkien's work may be productively viewed. Consecration Analysis may be an effective way of getting at the heart of *The Lord of the Rings*; but other approaches yield different conclusions than mine, and an examination of several of these is warranted.

This chapter, by necessity, will be a subjective general review of the literature representing several other paradigms. I am not likely to be objective in this review, because I fundamentally disagree with most of these approaches; I will endeavor, nonetheless, to be as charitable to their advocates as I can, describing the merits of such approaches while pointing out where my views differ. I will not, however, present full book reviews, instead focusing on the authors' own claims about their works.

I have subjectively grouped my review of the literature into three categories. The first is a collection of approaches which I believe are only marginally compelling; these we will cover only briefly. The second is a pair of approaches which appear to be very compelling to a wide audience: the somewhat pessimistic "Long Defeat" view discussed by both Tolkien and C. S. Lewis, and Joseph Pearce's "Required Reading" view; these will be discussed at length. The third grouping is that which I personally find the most useful, and includes a broad school of thought which I call the "Catholic Historical" view, and a popular approach which might be described as the "Ethics and Values" view.

THE MARGINALLY COMPELLING

"Egoistic instinct is subtle and glamorous," Booth Tarkington wrote. "It can even mistake itself for authoritative judgment upon works of art; but if we avoid being carried away by its eloquence we needn't share in its error. That is, by making ourselves a little hard-headed we can escape the confusion of mind that damns an ostrich for not being a giraffe."[1] The worst kind of chaff, Tarkington argues, is that which we bring to a work of art ourselves: one in which our own desires outweigh the intentions of the artist, and blind us to whatever legitimate merits may exist. There are many approaches to the *Lord of the Rings* which are particularly blind.

The least useful of these approaches, as we have already observed, is probably the reactionary response of

Christian conservatives. A perfect example would be David W. Cloud, writing on-line at *logosresourcepages.org*. A fellow minister of Christ, Mr. Cloud writes:

> "Is *The Lord of the Rings* harmless fantasy or perhaps even a wholesome Christian allegory? We think not. I read *The Hobbit* and the three volumes of *The Lord of the Rings* in 1971 when I was in Vietnam with the U.S. Army. I was not saved at the time, and, in fact, I was very antagonistic to the Christian faith; and had the books contained even a hint of Bible truth, I can assure you that I would not have read them at that particular point in my life. Though I have forgotten many of the details of the books, I can recall very vividly that they are filled with occultic imagery. The books were published in inexpensive paperback editions in the late 1960s, and they became very popular with that generation of drug headed hippies."[2]

Of course, ministers like Cloud, though meaning well, are terribly uninformed about their subject, and rely on anecdotal personal experience for their conclusions. While Cloud is correct that Tolkien's books may be a waste of time for those earnestly hungering after God's Word, his biased attacks on Tolkien aren't a legitimate path to that conclusion.

Perhaps on the opposite end of the spectrum is Bradley J. Birzer. An assistant professor of history at Hillsdale College and senior fellow with the Center for the American Idea in Houston, Birzer's book *J. R. R. Tolkien's Sanctifying Myth* presents itself as a fairly mainstream analysis. "Birzer situates Tolkien within the Christian humanist tradition represented by Thomas More and T. S. Eliot, Dante and C. S. Lewis," the book's publicity states. "He argues that through the genre of myth Tolkien is able to provide a sophisticated — and appealing — social and ethical worldview."[3]   Behind Birzer's thinking, however, is a rather extreme interpretation of Tolkien's opinions.

While Birzer is right in observing that Tolkien called the sudden appearance of "a dark figure, one of the nine Ringwraiths" in his story a divinely inspired event, Birzer makes a startling claim. "Tolkien firmly believed that his characters had existed long before he had, that God had given him the story," Birzer writes. "He believed he merely recorded it. Ultimately, Tolkien claimed, God was the true author of the *Silmarillion* and *The Lord of the Rings*."[4]

Such theories tend to provoke reactionary responses like Cloud's. I can find no clear basis for Birzer's assertions, and believe they present Tolkien in an unnecessarily controversial light.   It's just as plausible to interpret Tolkien's words as a form of artistic hyperbole resulting from his own "Secondary Belief."   Tolkien was only too aware of his own human chaff to truly consider God the author of his own very human work.

Of course, Birzer may himself be writing reactively, defending Tolkien's work against the same kind of mystical analysis which concerns Cloud. This willfully manipulative approach is represented in Gareth Knight's *The Magical World of J. R. R. Tolkien*.   Knight chooses to interpret Middle-Earth as a "complete realm of magical beings," a world whose "stories tap into the realms of far-memory and myth, giving access to treasures of wisdom and insight buried deep in the collective imagination." Not surprisingly, the book's jacket notes that Knight is "one of today's foremost writers on the subjects of Magic, the Qabalah, and the Western Mystery Tradition. He has devoted a lifetime to rediscovering and teaching the principles of esoteric philosophy and practice as a spiritual discipline and method of self-realization."[5]

Such a mystical treatment, then, may appeal to Knight because of his own metaphysical predispositions. But he is mistaken to interpret Tolkien in that light, and Birzer is right to point out that Tolkien's influences are Christian, by design, and not primarily pagan; certainly not neo-pagan.

But if one mistakenly assumes that Tolkien was virulently anti-modernist or proto-post-modernist one could draw any number of such conclusions. When one throws reason to the wind, one may easily throw caution with it. And so we find such conclusions as Roger Sale's baffling, politically-correct tolerant heroism for the modern age: "lonely, lost, scared, loving, willing, and compassionate," eager to "bind oneself to the otherness of others by recognizing our common livingness." Sale is only too quick to ignore Frodo's marked reluctance to tolerantly bind himself to the type of otherness exhibited by Boromir, Wormtongue, or even Ted Sandyman. Tolkien's universe is one in which a distinct moral order prevails, even if it is not rigidly codified. Tolkien is not greatly interested in politically correct celebration of diversity.

And when post-modernist Patrick Curry, in *Defending Middle-Earth*, can loosely argue that *The Lord of the Rings* was a manifesto for revolt against the values of modern society,[6] it becomes evident that Tolkien's meaning is as mutable as that of the Oracle of Delphi. The reader is likely indeed to find in Middle-Earth what the reader brings to it. Tolkien's fans have even felt entirely free to do that which the author himself decried: turning Middle-Earth into an escapist paradise. "Can the singer enter into his tale or the designer into his picture?"[7] asks Andreth, somewhat rhetorically, in the Dialog. As we have seen, Tolkien responded definitively in the negative. "Hobbits are not a Utopian vision, or recommended as an ideal in their own or any age,"[8] Tolkien wrote in 1954.

But the publication of *The Lord of the Rings*, as we all know, has been influential in spawning any number of escapist enterprises: Dungeons and Dragons, creative anachronism, the remote youth hostel "Rivendell" on Scotland's Western shores, even recent cryptic reports out of Australia and Russia indicating organization of religious and political movements based on Tolkien's writings. "I am not now at all sure that the tendency to treat the whole thing as a kind of vast game is really good," Tolkien wrote, long before escapist appreciation of his art had become excessive. For his own part, Tolkien found "that kind of thing only too fatally attractive."[9]

So why are Tolkien's readers so drawn into Middle-Earth? Don't they know better? One might as well ask: Why do people smoke when they should know better? Why do people throw money away gambling when they should know better? Why do folks with Jesus fish on their cars speed when they should know better? Unfortunately, Tolkien's world is not one that places much premium on "knowing better." Tolkien's characters do all kinds of things that they know is not good for them, even Wizards such as Saruman. For escapists, perhaps that is part of Middle-Earth's appeal.

If none of these views stands up well to rational scrutiny, however, we can be sure that a strictly humanist approach is also deficient. There is more to Frodo and Company than an affirmation that "individual human beings are the fundamental source of all value and have the ability to understand — and perhaps even to control — the natural world by careful application of their own rational faculties."[10] Tolkien's *dénouement* certainly stresses personal responsibility; but it is tempered both by a genuine faith in providence and a certain darkness: pessimism about the process of living, and about the ultimate success of rationality.

THE LONG DEFEAT?

A great number of readers and critics do not interpret Tolkien's *dénouement* as pessimistic at all, merely realistic. The most noted opinion on the subject is, of course, Tolkien's own. As we have seen during our discussion of Tolkien's faith, he believed that the story of human history is a story of "the long defeat," in the words of Galadriel. Oddly, he attributed this view to his status as a "Christian, and indeed a Roman Catholic." But such a view is not uniquely Catholic. Lewis, a Protestant, was also sympathetic to this dark view, seeing the moral of Tolkien's story as the middle-ground between "facile optimism" and "wailing pessimism": the "hard, yet not quite desperate, insight" that "every time we win we shall know that our victory is impermanent."

The origins of this view are difficult to trace, but may be most fully explicated in the writings of the influential 19th-century American thinker Ralph Waldo Emerson. A Unitarian minister, Emerson wrote prolifically on a broad range of topics, and spoke explicitly of the "long defeat."[11] In his essay "Inspiration," Emerson writes that the human experience itself is "a flash of light, then a long darkness, then a flash again."[12] Hence, the darkness is relative; it is the curse of Adam. To be human is to live in the absence of God's presence, and to die is to return. All human pursuit, as Solomon expresses so eloquently in Ecclesiastes, is vain — "a long way leading nowhere,"[13] as Emerson put it.

Emerson understood this long darkness as compatible with providence. He noted that the "wars which make history so dreary have served the cause of truth and virtue. There is always an instinctive sense of right, an obscure idea... which in long periods vindicates itself at last."[14] Certainly, these are the terms under which Tolkien would have understood the War of the Ring. Tom Shippey, author of *J. R. R. Tolkien: Author of the Century*, agrees. "Middle-Earth demonstrates the need for Christianity," he asserts. He believes that Tolkien's work reveals that in its absence, "the whole of history will only be 'the long defeat.'"[15]

Still, interpreting from this view allows one to observe, as does critic Edmund Fuller, that in "both the Third Age and our world, evil is never defeated once for all."[16] If we agree with Emerson's disciple, Thoreau, that most of us "lead lives of quiet desperation,"[17] the Long Defeat view will not be greatly encouraging to many; and while it may mesh nicely with Solomon's thinking, there is something "greater than Solomon"[18] in the person and teaching of Christ.

In what Scriptural terms is the struggle between good and evil stated? Is it fair to say that it is really a struggle, as much as a foregone conclusion simply being worked out one day at a time, with the powerful assistance of our Maker? "Who shall separate us from the love of Christ? Shall trouble or hardship or persecution or famine or nakedness or danger or sword?"[19] To view life as a struggle or long defeat may over time persuade us that the outcome is in doubt. It is not. And, to be fair, the Long Defeat view does not really make that claim. However, it would perhaps be better to live in confident assurance, as the Apostle Paul states, that "we are more than conquerors through him who loved us. For I am convinced that neither death nor life, neither angels nor demons, neither the present nor the future, nor any powers, neither height nor depth, nor anything else in all creation, will be able to separate us from the love of God that is in Christ Jesus our Lord."[20] It is in the love of Christ, in this life, that we find victory, not only in the promised Return and resurrection to new life. Living in

Confident Victory is perhaps more compelling than living in Long Defeat. As a man thinks, says the proverb, "so is he."[21]

Can we accept that life is joyous perseverance in the face of suffering, that God does not ask us to do more than we can bear and that there is only *apparent* struggle? And if we accept this, what is the implication, then, of our human inclination to see all things as symbolic of a struggle which doesn't really exist? Perhaps we can move from a black and white world into simply a white world with misunderstood shadows. In the former, black must be feared and defeated; in the latter, white need only shine its light to reveal the good in all things. The illusion of darkness is simply that: an illusion and a deceit which must be exposed, not expunged.

I am sure that Lewis would accuse me of facile optimism; but I do live in the real world, and my confidence in God's victory over the power of sin in this life has not gone unrewarded. And in the end, our analysis of *The Lord of the Rings* has shown that Tolkien also felt that the darkness of the Fourth Age was excessive, and oppressive. Middle-Earth needed our Savior, and it didn't have Him.

REQUIRED READING?

Probably the most widely read and popular analysis of *The Lord of the Rings* is Joseph Pearce's *Tolkien: Man and Myth*. In the Preface to this book, I referenced his assertion "that Tolkien's epic should be required reading in every Christian family. It should take its place beside the Narnian Chronicles of C. S. Lewis (Tolkien's great friend) and the fairy stories of George Macdonald as an indispensable part of a Christian childhood."[22] To be entirely fair, I must point out that Pearce has made this remark in response to groundless prohibitory cautions against Tolkien's work. But I believe Pearce's reactive, defensive position leads him to err in his assertion.

Pearce's analysis of Tolkien, however, is possibly the most complete and accurate yet published. His greatest contribution is a sober examination of the underinformed and misinformed popular response to Tolkien's fiction. "He may be the most popular writer of our age," the book's jacket notes, "but Tolkien is often misunderstood."[23] Pearce, writer in residence at Ave Maria College, is right on the mark when noting that "Tolkien has no time for the amoral relativism that is so prevalent in much of what passes as modern entertainment."[24] As we have seen, Tolkien's glimpses of truth are intended to point to a specific, concrete Truth. And Pearce puts this observation in its appropriate cultural context. "The fact that Tolkien's myth contains more truth than most of what passes as realism," he notes, "serves as a damning indictment of the false vision being presented by today's mass media."[25]

Yet Pearce is given to defensive, gentle hyperbole. For instance, he boldly claims in interviews that "there is no doubt that *The Lord of the Rings* is a profoundly Christian myth."[26] The position is arguable, yes, and even compellingly so; but we have seen that it is also arguable that myths which merely point to Christ are not Christian, but pre-Christian. Judaism is not "profoundly Christian." It's profoundly Jewish.

Pearce is also able to claim that the values which "emerge in *The Lord of the Rings* are the values that emerge in the Gospels."[27] True, Tolkien's characters exhibit *many* of the Christian virtues in their actions, attitudes and beliefs. But where are many of the other virtues expressed, for example, in the Sermon on the Mount? Who are Middle-Earth's peacemakers? Who eschews resistance to evil?

Who turns the other cheek? Who loves their enemies, and prays for them instead of killing them? Again, I reveal my facile optimism, I suppose. Pearce asks, "How can Christians possibly object to a quest, the purpose of which is to thwart the evil designs of the demonic enemy?"[28] I reply: The ends do not justify the means. The War of the Ring may be conducted on terms which are realistic in our own world, but those terms are not unilaterally understood as Christlike.

Pearce's position is, of course, heavily influenced by a Thomist understanding of Just War Theory. "As developed by Augustine and Aquinas, just war theory typically distinguishes the conditions under which war may be initiated (*ius ad bellum*), including a legitimate authority exercising a right intention in pursuit of a just cause, from the rules under which war may be conducted (*ius in bello*), including concern with proportionality of the means and discrimination between combatants and non-combatants."[29] It's worth noting, again, that a perfunctory dismissal of Aquinas would be ill-advised. At the same time, it's also worth noting that there is a compelling argument to be made for pacifism as well. Neither view should be summarily dismissed and neither is essential to the gospel.

Still, Pearce's hyperbole may not reflect his true intentions, and it's possible that his audience may misunderstand him. For instance, willful readers may take his assertion that it is a "story's truth, not its facts, that matter"[30] to mean that the fact of the resurrection is not as important as its truth. Such a conclusion would appall Pearce; and if we really believe that *The Lord of the Rings* is required reading in our households, we go too far. The only book which is required reading for Christians is the Bible, and we spend far too little of our time immersed in that book as it is.

Pearce is not alone, of course. There are a great many folk who see *The Lord of the Rings* as an indispensable demonstration of Christian thought. I neither see it as indispensable nor fully demonstrative. I don't believe Tolkien did, either.

CATHOLIC HISTORICISM

Pearce is, of course, writing from a distinctly Roman Catholic perspective. So was Tolkien. As many readers at Hollywood Jesus pointed out, my Protestant American non-confessional non-liturgical non-denominational Restoration Movement background makes me ill-qualified to discuss the specifically Catholic elements of Tolkien's work. To an extent, the observation is justified; and I have been eternally blessed by the patient endeavors of several of my Roman Catholic brethren and their forbearance in our lengthy correspondence.

I will not here attempt a thorough Catholic explication of *The Lord of the Rings*. Joseph Pearce's work should satisfy those desiring such an analysis. Instead, I will review three topics which appear consistently in theological debates about Tolkien's works, and ones which seem foundational to the historic development of post-Renaissance thought in the Roman Catholic Church: Christian humanism, natural law and salvation history. An understanding of these issues illuminates one of the more compelling interpretations of *The Lord of the Rings*.

Christian humanism, first, must be differentiated from *humanism*. The latter is "an educational and philosophical outlook that emphasizes the personal worth of the individual and the central importance of human values as opposed to religious belief."[31] It originated in the western rediscovery, during the Renaissance, of ancient Greek and Latin literature and philosophy. Humanism was, in fact, behind the cultural revolution which produced the enlightenment and modern thought. It was not characterized, however, by an openness to metaphysical speculation; and by the 18th century, humanism "had come to be identified with a purely secular attitude — one that often rejected Christianity altogether."[32]

Today, the term *humanism* has come to mean many things to many people. "In the works of the pragmatist philosopher Ferdinand Schiller," summarizes Benjamin G. Kohl, "humanism is seen as that philosophical understanding which stems from human activity. Irving Babbitt used the word to describe a program of reaction against romanticism and naturalism in literature. Jean Paul Sartre developed a scientific humanism preaching human worth based on Marxist theory."[33] Further, the American Humanist Association, which sprang from the Unitarian Church to which Emerson belonged, "holds that human beings can satisfy religious needs from within, discarding the concept of God as inconsistent with advanced thought and human freedom."[34]

So these humanist teachings are those to which conservative Christians refer, in an incensed and fearful way, as *secular humanism.* Christian humanism, on the other hand, grew out of the religious philosophy of Thomas Aquinas, and later interpretation by Jacques Maritain. Today, Christian humanists point to the Incarnation as demonstration of the importance of the individual, and see it as affirmation of the Old Covenant's revelation that man was created in God's image. Christian humanists further assert "that the worth of the individual is a consistent theme in the teaching of Jesus." While they acknowledge their indebtedness to the general philosophical tradition of humanism, Christian humanists "caution that these other forms can degenerate into excessive individualism or savage collectivism because they operate without God. The Christian humanist values culture but confesses that man is fully developed only as he comes into a right relationship with Christ."[35]

Closely related is Aquinas' theory of natural law. Thomists understand the principles of human morality as entirely within the domain of human reason. God has given humans their unique nature, the argument goes, and has designed man to come to a saving understanding of Him and His purposes through a rational nature. The Apostle Paul employed such an understanding when addressing the church in Rome: "what may be known about God is plain" to man "because God has made it plain" in understandable ways. "Since the creation of the world," Paul explains, "God's invisible qualities — his eternal power and divine nature — have been clearly seen, being understood from what has been made, so that men are without excuse."[36]

Further, while the mind of man cannot "know the eternal law, as it is in itself," Aquinas argues that man can apprehend it "in its reflection, greater or less"; that is, natural law is "a kind of reflection and participation of eternal law."[37] James J. Fox explains:

"The eternal law is God's wisdom, inasmuch as it is the directive norm of all movement and action. When God willed to give existence to creatures, He willed to ordain and direct them to an end. In the case of inanimate things, this Divine direction is provided for in the nature which God has given to each; in them determinism reigns. Like all the rest of creation, man is destined by God to an end, and receives from Him a direction towards this end. This ordination is of a character in harmony with his free intelligent nature. In virtue of his intelligence and free will, man is master of his conduct. Unlike the things of the mere material world he can vary his action, act, or abstain from action, as he pleases. Yet he is not a lawless being in an ordered universe. In the very constitution of his nature, he too has a law laid down for him, reflecting that ordination and direction of all things, which is the eternal law. The rule, then, which God has prescribed for our conduct, is found in our nature itself. Those actions which conform with its tendencies, lead to our destined end, and are thereby constituted right and morally good; those at variance with our nature are wrong and immoral."[38]

To an extent, Gandalf expounds this Thomist doctrine when explaining that the individual's role is to decide "what to do with the time that is given us." This presumes, of course, that our actions are consistent with what God has revealed to us of His will.

Salvation history puts natural law squarely in subjection to providence. It "presupposes that divine powers direct historical processes and events toward certain results." From this perspective, "God's plan for humans works itself out through a complicated but ever-ongoing process that moves slowly toward God's goals."[39] The mechanism is a Christian humanist exercise of the rational free will of every created being, each acting in accordance with inescapable natural law, to fulfill the larger purposes of God's grand designs, even when we freely and sinfully act contrary to natural law.

Such understandings yield a different spiritual perspective for the Roman Catholic. Regina Doman summarizes the contrast between Protestant and Catholic views of history. "From a Protestant's point of view," she says,

"The world was dark, and then Christ came into the

world with His light. Christ's light spread throughout the world. The world fought back against this
light. Martyrs died, blood was shed, and in the end,
Christ conquered. So the Enemy spread poison to
fight against Christ — this poison was twisting doctrines and loosening morals. Christ's truth was corrupted and people were Christian in name, but in
reality their souls were dark and damned. Then one
man saw the light, and by God's grace, fought
against the twisted mess of aged corruption and old
dead traditions, and brought a new day on the face of
the earth. Martyrs died, blood was shed, but in the
end, Christ conquered. The Enemy always uses the
same strategy — twisting doctrine, corrupting
morals, but every time, Christ's followers will have
the courage to leave the past behind and go forward,
always forward, out of Babylon, toward the future,
ascending into the time when God's Kingdom will
come on earth as Christ returns. Martyrs may die,
blood will be shed, but Christ cannot be conquered."

"The history of Christianity from a Catholic's point of
view," says Doman, "specifically a Catholic in modern
Protestant England," is very different.

"The world was dark, and then Christ came
into the world with His light. Christ suffered and
died for us, shed his blood. He founded a Church,
gave the sacraments, chose apostles and bade them
to be faithful to Him and to teach His flock on earth.
He ascended into glory and His apostles, empowered by the Spirit, went forth to teach the world. The
darkness fought against the Church. The Church
suffered, and martyrs died, and after years, the
Church conquered the Roman empire. Her Enemy
was treacherous and used many snares, but in the

end, the empire was Christian.

"Then the barbarian tide washed over it and it was gone, and with it much learning, much that was beautiful was lost. But the Church was not daunted. Once again she built up a civilization: baptized, taught, gave the sacraments, built hospitals, established schools, formed, excommunicated, exorcised, shaped barbarian civilization into a new Christian civilization — vast and ordered, where learning was preserved, slavery was outlawed, women were honored, and beautiful works of art were built up to glorify God.

"Then the Enemy sent another tide, another religion, Islam, to devastate and destroy. And the Church fought, and in some places won, but much was lost. Whole peoples suffered, died. Works of beauty were lost forever, parts of the world that had been Christian sank into barbarism. Evangelization was hindered, zeal faltered. The tide was turned in Spain, and the Christian civilization went on.

"But cracks in the moral foundation of the clergy widened and men were impatient for reform, and instead turned their fury on the Church that had brought them up. Political alliances were made, and whole nations lost the Faith, turning instead to a debased form of Christianity, harsh and pitiless. Works of art were destroyed. Ignorance was praised. Centuries of tradition were cast aside carelessly. Much that was precious was lost, whole nations lost their birthright of the Church.

"Then the descendants of those who had left the Church rebuked Christianity — Christ as well as the Church. Darkness fell on the Western mind in the Enlightenment. Terror came to France in the form of atheistic revolution, sowing seeds that would blossom gruesomely in Russia in the 20th century. Where men had praised God they now scorned Him as irrelevant. Italy seized the papal states. England crushed Catholic Ireland. Those Catholics in England who remained are a tiny remnant, weak, remembering the past but too frustrated and disunited to do little more than remember. The darkness of atheism stalks the world. Everywhere the Church is beset on all sides. She is always haunted by her own weaknesses.

"Yes, we know that Christ will return, and this is our hope. But before the Resurrection is always the Cross. We fear our own Golgotha. We are in the Garden of Olives, and we hear the footfalls of the Betrayer."

"See the difference?" she asks in closing. "Doesn't this second history read an awful lot like *The Silmarillion?*"[40] And she's right. It does.

From this Catholic historical perspective, we may understand the actions of Frodo and his friends as entirely faithful, to the extent that Eru has revealed himself to them. We may also understand even the actions of Gollum and the Witch King of Angmar as demonstrating the cooperation of natural law with God's purposes. And we may see the entirety of Tolkien's fiction as an ostensibly historical episode consistent with actual salvation history.

The Catholic historical perspective is important in understanding the easy embrace of Catholics for *The Lord of the Rings*. For many of them, Christian humanism, natural law and salvation history are readily apparent in Tolkien's story. Understanding this perspective may also prove especially compelling for Protestants, many of whom may never have heard of these teachings.

Still, if we substitute a purely monotheistic human-ism for a Christian humanism, we may observe that any rational being with an appreciation for providence could easily see the same themes in *The Lord of the Rings*. Such ideas are not uniquely Christian. But understood in light of Christ, they become unique.

ETHICS AND VALUES

I do find the intellectual rigor which my Catholic brethren apply to Tolkien's fiction a refreshing alternative to the rather gentle, direct approach taken by popular evangel-ical Protestant analysts. Intervarsity Press, for instance, offers a volume titled *Tolkien's Ordinary Virtues: Exploring the Spiritual Themes of The Lord of the Rings*, by Mark Eddy Smith. The title alone explains that we won't be dig-ging too deep into the theology of Tolkien's world. The book cover also serves as the shirt sleeve upon which Smith's emotional approach is prominently worn. The "mere recollection" of Frodo's sacrificial pledge at Rivendell, he tells us, can move him "to tears."[41] Okay, for me, it's "Fly, you fools!" at Khazad-dûm. But I'm not at all sure that "it moves me" is in itself a recommendation for spiritual nourishment.

And it isn't for Smith, either. "As I get older, and learn more of what sort of person I am, and continue sojourning to the rich soil of the Shire and the high towers of Minas Tirith," he continues, "I discover that many of my notions of what is good and right and noble in this world have their source in that one."[42] Well, that's interesting. Can you tell us more? "*The Lord of the Rings* offers us the essential lessons in living," Smith's book claims. "Here we discover ordinary virtues, like generosity, pity, hospitality and rest. We meet extraordinary people, like Bilbo, Gandalf, Tom Bombadil and Glorfindel. We learn about the roots of destruction in pride and betrayal. And we find the ingredients for success, such as community and sacrifice."[43]

It sounds like a more noble version of *Friends*, *Cheers*, or a weekend with my whacked-out but very Christian poker buddies. Still, Smith's book isn't done. There's more. "Each of us — even the most simple — is called to a journey. We may be asked to leave behind everything we have grown dependent on. And when this is the case, the tale of Frodo and his friends offers hope that we will be given the strength and the help we need to overcome every obstacle and defeat every foe. This book will help you find the way."[44]

Of course, Smith doesn't really mean to imply that *The Lord of the Rings* is our true source of hope and strength. "Reading (or writing) about the virtues of fictional characters," Smith rightly observes, "has little power to instill those virtues in us."[45] The very ordinary virtues found in Tolkien's novel do have Scripture and God as their source; and Smith really hopes that those hungering and thirsting after Middle-Earth can be introduced to more nourishing spiritual appetites through this kind of values analysis. In the end, Smith knows, "the primary virtue of *The Lord of the Rings* is storytelling."[46]

To be honest, the movie and book reviews published on David Bruce's Hollywood Jesus take the same, relentlessly positive, approach as Smith. It's commendable, and worth trying. If one is accustomed to employing a hard-nosed, provocative, cynical approach, like I used to be, one may be transformed into the Pollyanna-esque facile optimist I have apparently become.

Okay, I haven't made the transition entirely yet,

because I still feel this approach has its pitfalls. But Kurt D. Bruner and Jim Ware, in Tyndale House's *Finding God in the Lord of the Rings*, are a little more sober in their similar treatment. While they also, like Smith, see that Tolkien's books "offer a rich tapestry of redemption, values, and faith against all odds from which we may learn much," they are up front in pointing out that the books were never intended "to present the gospel," and are best reviewed "in the light of Scripture."[47]

Bruner and Ware's review of Tolkien's work is light and airy, however, and never really approaches any significant theological issues. The light touch is also characteristic of a certain myopia. "I think only someone with a Christian understanding of the world could have written" *The Lord of the Rings*, Bruner says, "because he understands that evil is real, it is personal and it is possessing."[48] Christians all too often presume that we have cornered the market on ethics and moral values; but Jews and Muslims, among many many others, also know that evil is real, personal and possessing. Titles such as *Finding Allah in The Lord of the Rings* or *Tolkien: A Patriarchal Perspective* might soon appear at *Amazon.com*, and they would be no less legitimate than Bruner and Ware's book.

So an "ethics and values" approach to Tolkien's works, especially when guided by the authority of Scripture, can indeed be rewarding and profitable. But the approach does ignore Tolkien's more serious intentions, and can come off as trite or glib. It may also lead to the false impression that Jesus preached a purely ethical gospel, and it never raises any serious concerns about Christians like myself or Mark Eddy Smith who claim to have read *The Lord of the Rings* a dozen times. At present, in my own life, there is still a great deal of evidence that my allegiance to Tolkien may be more important to me than my allegiance to

Scripture; and this may badly color my own perceptions.

Until this very human, earthenware pot has read the Bible through more times than *The Silmarillion*, I won't be calling Smith's kettle black, or anyone else's. I'll simply have to content myself with trying to persuade us all that being scorched by the cooking fire is undesirable. And when I get to the point where I can't stand the heat, I'll get out of the kitchen.

SO WHY BOTHER?

Another of the terrific inquiries spawned by Hollywood Jesus wanted to know what the fuss was all about. Why, the reader wanted to know, do long-winded fools like me bother with such extensive, detailed analyses of stuff like *The Lord of the Rings* and *Harry Potter?* "We bother to do the things we find interesting," I replied (rather than taking the hint and *not bothering* to respond, or simply getting a grip on myself). "Others need not find it interesting. And when they don't," I continued, with my typing fingers firmly in my cheek, "it's not incumbent upon them to bother to remark. Why bother to comment on something you don't find worth the bother? Because you find it interesting."

People who write books like this one — or Birzer's, Pearce's or Smith's — and people who read them happen to be interested. Of course, answering the question, "why do we *bother*?" is not nearly as interesting as answering the question, "why are we *interested*?" Further, *should* we be interested? And if so, why, and to what purpose?

Chapter Eight

CONCLUSIONS: GOLD, OR JUST GLITTER?

All that is gold does not glitter,

Not all those who wander are lost;

The old that is strong does not wither,

Deep roots are not reached by the frost.[1]

With these words, Gandalf provides Frodo an introduction to his guide and protector, Aragorn. Forget his
rough appearance: Strider is much more than he appears.

Tolkien's verse is a variation on an old saw, the
aphorism which observes, "Not all that glitters is gold." So
in our search for spiritual gold, we must also remember that
appearances can be deceiving. Often, we may be attracted
by the glitter of fool's gold; and just as often, we may miss
the value of unrefined ore. In our passion for discovering a
motherlode, we may also disdainfully pass over scattered
traces of filament as not worth our while. Other prospec-
tors may enrich themselves at the expense of our haste.
"Humanity is not incidentally engaged, but eternally and
systematically engaged," Chesterton observed, "in throwing
gold into the gutter and diamonds into the sea."[2]

A seasoned prospector, immune to the lust of gold
fever, knows that gold is found in many forms, and in many
unexpected contexts. Gold is also rarely found in its purest
form: Ore must be assayed to determine its purity. Then the
prospector may determine whether the cost of extracting

gold from the ore can be justified. And there will be no unrealistic expectation that only pure gold is worth mining.

The only pure gold for the Christian, of course, is God's Word itself. We would be foolish to presume that we will find any purer source. We may turn to specialists to help extract the gold of Scripture from the bedrock; we may even find that veins of less pure ore are connected to God's motherlode; and we may be enriched by panning for placer within the watershed of God's mountain. But we must be ever cognizant that whatever truth we do find leads back to the pure vein of Scripture. And we must be increasingly vigilant about the attractiveness of iron pyrite the further we wander from the True Source.

So what do we find in *The Lord of the Rings*? How pure is the ore we find there, and how closely related is it to the motherlode? Such questions are the object of Consecration Analysis. At the outset, we hoped to answer three questions with regard to *intent* and *artifact*. First: is there evidence that Tolkien's purposes were with Christ, or at least not against Him? Second, is there evidence that Tolkien's fiction is consistent with what we know of his purposes? And finally, what concerns may need to be addressed so that we may honor God through our own handling of Tolkien's work?

Hopefully, we have seen that *The Lord of the Rings* is no mere story. It is simply the most visible element of a grand and complex myth, and there is great power in Tolkien's mythology. If it were not powerful, it would not be popular. Hence, to the public mind, the T-mythology is terribly relevant. One of the major reasons for its relevance is its warm embrace of a metaphysical universe, and a rejection of the more damaging aspects of a rational, mechanistic view.

So post-modernism is decidedly a factor in the present power of Tolkien's fiction. But that's not entirely by design, as we have seen, because Tolkien was not, properly speaking, anti-modernist. For Tolkien, fantasy "does not destroy or even insult Reason."[3] While we may excitedly embrace his fiction as a means of connecting with a post-modern desire for meaning beyond barren rationality, for Tolkien the solution was neither modernity nor a knee-jerk response to it, but faith.

Oddly enough, the powerful relevance of Middle-Earth is not found in a distinctly Christian world view but a deliberately pre-Christian world view. Tolkien was remarkably prescient in seeing that what our modern world needed was a new pre-Christian mythology, a new story to point the world to Christ — not to replace the True Story, but to point the way back for disenfranchised or disillusioned seekers. This is tremendously good news for those who are passionate about reaching the lost in today's society. If Tolkien's myth is powerfully popular due to its pre-Christian design, then clearly we have a widespread, pre-Christian cultural movement afoot. As we will see presently, this puts the ball squarely in our court; and we'd best not drop it.

At the same time, Tolkien was aware of the chaff in his corn. What hope is there for a Fourth Age Believer? What does Middle-Earth's metaphysics have to offer, in a concrete way, for one of "the Atani," or as Andreth's people call themselves, "the Seekers"? Man is the race of Middle-Earth which "journeyed west in vain hope," and finds the journey "mere flight in a dream from what waking they know."[4] Tolkien was aware that, without Christ, Seekers are left to search in fallen darkness, clinging to vague hopes but never living in abundant, saving Christian faith. He also knew that such a faith was not portrayed in *The Lord of the*

Rings.

There is too much "long defeat" in Middle-Earth, and not enough confident victory. Tolkien's Fourth Age, as we find it in *The Lord of the Rings*, is even devoid of the providential aid provided for the War of the Ring. How can a Seeker, or even a believing Christian, be transformed by the renewing of the mind if the mind itself is convinced that the supernatural is beyond human experience? The mind must be positively engaged, must fervently believe, so that the Spirit may triumph. The greatest danger of Tolkien's fantasy lies not in seduction to the "dark side" of spirituality, but in a misguided conclusion: that we may find our own spiritual condition accurately mirrored in that of the Fourth Age Believer — and that we are just as hopeless.

Fortunately, as Edmund Fuller observes (and we have already seen), Tolkien's "wonder tale is rich with teaching for life as *we* lead it."[5] And the answer to potential misinterpretation of Middle-Earth's spirituality lies in Tolkien's fiction, which is itself a Thomist expression of the role which personal responsibility plays in bringing about God's purposes. It is up to us to determine how we spend the time God has allotted us, as Gandalf says. And if we know we should journey to Mount Doom, then go we must.

That is, if we are aware of the tremendous popularity of Tolkien's work, and the parching thirst for spiritual meaning which is behind that popularity; and if Tolkien himself has provided us with an understanding of how a Seeker may be pointed to Christ, we have only ourselves to blame if *The Lord of the Rings* is somehow turned to harm for ourselves or those we know. What we should find truly interesting is not Tolkien's work, but God's work; and in the case of the T-mythology, how we may best turn Tolkien's own work to that end. "Anyone, then, who knows the good he ought to do and doesn't do it," warns the Bible, "sins."[6]

NEXT STEPS

So how do we, as Christian Tolkien fans, go about wielding Tolkien's powerful fiction in a responsible manner? The answer to that question comes in three flavors: one for ourselves, one for our fellow Christians, and one for nonbelievers.

For ourselves, we must first be convicted of the power of Christ's victory over death; we must then start living as though we really value that victory; and we must accept some responsibility for the spiritual state of our fellow man. Many Christians have allowed Middle-Earth to become an escapist substitute for the true consolation of God's Word. Many more habitually allow other distractions and the cares of the world to snatch away what true seed has managed to find its way into their hearts. And unfortunately, the vast majority exhibit little or no appreciation for their role as ambassadors to a dying world.

Scripture advises, however, that we be fully convinced of God's ability to accomplish far more than we as humans could conceive. At the risk of facile optimism, we need to live in confident assurance that Christ, in the resurrection, has already won the final victory; and that His church will prevail, in both this world and the next. In practice, we rarely live out our faith in a way that demonstrates this confidence. As a result, we fail to fully immerse ourselves in Kingdom culture. Our daily walk, even our strategies for bolstering our faith, are unfortunately sullied by worldly philosophies. If we are to communicate the joy of the gospel to others, it must be evidenced in our own lives, and we must live as though we truly believe it.

What does this mean in a practical sense, particularly with respect to *The Lord of the Rings*? For starters, we must realize that what we consume tells us a great deal about our true appetites. Which do we read more, the Bible, or Tolkien's fiction? Now, we're not talking about the ancillary benefits of "Bible study" here, which are many and profound. We're talking about reading for enjoyment. Do we really enjoy reading Scripture? Does it satisfy the desires of our heart? If not, why not? Because we don't really know what's good for us. It is a sad but very true fact that the Bible is actually much shorter in length than the combined length of *The Hobbit*, *The Lord of the Rings* and *The Silmarillion*. And it is also sad but very true that Scripture contains not only the wonderful virtues expressed in Tolkien's fiction but so many more. Further, and more importantly, it contains the powerful saving message of the death, burial and resurrection of Jesus, the Christ, as the final price for the sins of the world.

Scripture is the inspired Word of God, and contains within it the power to save a man's soul; but somehow, we exhibit little hunger or thirst for it. Instead of the bread of life, we hunger after a twinkie. For some, *The Lord of the Rings* may be the twinkie. Other twinkies abound. "Men have not only conceived of elves, but they have imagined gods, and worshipped them," Tolkien wrote. Men's false gods include "their notions, their banners, their monies; even their sciences and their social and economic theories have demanded human sacrifice."[7]

So we must agree to lay aside the twinkies, wherever we may find them, and commit to a steady diet of bread. At first it will be difficult. We need to cultivate an appetite for the true bread. And when we find that we have our dietary problem under control, we can feel free to indulge in a twinkie from time to time. Until then, we've got to lay off.

Escapism may easily become idolatry. From what, after all, do we feel we must escape? And to what do we turn for consolation? The answers to these questions are certainly related to our appetites; but they are also more complicated than that. As Christians, we know that God has designed each of us with a unique purpose. He has also fully equipped each of us with the necessary means of sustanance while we fulfill that purpose. And certainly, rest and relaxation are a necessary part of that sustenance.

Escapism is not. If we desire to "escape," that means we feel trapped. How can we possibly feel trapped by God's purposes? It's not God's fault if we feel that way. It's ours. It's because, as broken, fallen human beings, we rely too much on our own understanding, our own misguided desires and our own strength. If the Apostle Paul, and countless other saints over the millennia, could rejoice even under the most squalid circumstances, there is little from which we should feel a legitimate need for escape. Indeed, under far less trying circumstances than the cloud of witnesses who preceded us, we live unbalanced and uncentered lives, constantly scrambling in quiet desperation. That's not God's design. He has much more in store for us; and the remedy may be found not in Middle-Earth or the other twinkies in the box, but in God's Word, in prayer and in purposeful fellowship — God-directed partnership, not just social intercourse — with other believers. We're not going to be much help to others if we're spiritual basket cases ourselves.

Our perceived need for escape, after all, may simply be symptomatic of our fallenness. There may be no need for escape, merely recovery of true sight. As Chesterton observed,

This is the great fall, the fall by which the fish forgets the sea, the ox forgets the meadow, the clerk forgets the city, every man forgets his environment and, in the fullest and most literal sense, forgets himself. This is the real fall of Adam, and it is a spiritual fall. ... Most probably we are in Eden still. It is only our eyes that have changed.[8]

If our faith has become trite or tired, it is only because it has become "like the things which once attracted us by their glitter," Tolkien says; "we laid hands on them, and we locked them in our hoard, acquired them, and acquiring them ceased to look at them."[9] Let us look our faith square in the face. God is convinced that we are precisely where He needs us to be; why can't we be likewise convinced?

We may then look expectantly to the future. Winning God's battles in this life is not up to us alone, fortunately. He has provided us with tremendous, even miraculous, spiritual aid. God does not want us living with some nostalgic longing for the supposed past, when Good was Good and Evil was Evil; nor does He want us entirely reliant on ourselves to work out our personal problems and social ills. Rather, He wants us living confidently in our hope for the future (a hope explicitly absent from Middle-Earth), reliant on Him and the power of His Spirit to accomplish through us more than we could possibly ask or imagine.[10] Let us live dynamically in the present, with great gratitude for the past, in confidence that the best lies yet in the future.

For our fellow workers in Christ, we may offer several sound pieces of advice. Those who have elected to take a vocal stand against *The Lord of the Rings*, for instance, need our assistance. These brethren are either uninformed, don't understand the ability of faith to sanctify art, or have stumbled through misunderstanding. Now, it's tempting to think of these brothers as "closed-minded Christians" or to conclude that they just don't matter. They don't have to read or even enjoy the books, and nobody's forcing them to. But they do matter, because they are part of the public dialog, and our dialog is a witness to the world.

Now, if these folks need "fixing," that's purely between them and God. But we all can, and should, be educated — and we all can be encouraged to express our opinions in a Christlike manner. We may then attempt to demonstrate that *The Lord of the Rings* represents no threat whatsoever to Christianity: "If God is for us, who can be against us?"[11] We all need to be reminded that fear or condemnation are not loving responses to anything or anyone.

We also need to encourage all of our brothers and sisters to be more discerning in their entertainment. The Scriptures themselves urge the exercise of discernment, and we all need to be more like the Bereans. We need to be willing to engage our popular entertainment with our minds, and take responsibility for the relative levels of corn and chaff we consume. We shall then even-handedly assess *The Lord of the Rings*, *Buffy the Vampire Slayer*, *Left Behind*, *The Simpsons* and *The Omega Code*.

Fellow Christians who have not yet approached Middle-Earth, however, do not need our hearty recommendation of *The Lord of the Rings*. What they do need is bold encouragement to immerse themselves in the only work that is truly Christian: the Bible. We dare not, in good conscience, presume that we are all called to invest time and energy in Middle-Earth; nor should we unilaterally endorse the consumption of the vast bookshelf published as *The History of Middle-Earth* for those who have already indulged. Tolkien's ore does not assay well enough to warrant such an investment, especially if we believe that time is short, and that what we do on a daily basis truly matters in God's Kingdom.

Those who have investigated *The Lord of the Rings* and found it dark and depressing also need our understanding. We are all at differing levels of spiritual resilience, and response to Tolkien's work will vary accordingly. Those who fail to find the story uplifting or encouraging may still be affirmed, particularly in light of the violence and darkness of Tolkien's tale. For others, *The Lord of the Rings* may be what the earthquake was for the Philippian jailer.

CONSIDERING OTHERS MORE IMPORTANT

"A theologian takes God seriously. A poet takes words seriously," Eugene Peterson is reported to have said. "A pastor takes actual persons seriously."[12] If we recall God's words to Ezekiel, we will remember that our obligations to the lost are significant indeed. Not surprisingly, one of God's most urgent pastoral directives was also recorded by Ezekiel:

> "Because my flock lacks a shepherd and so has been plundered and has become food for all the wild animals, and because my shepherds did not search for my flock but cared for themselves rather than for my flock, therefore, O shepherds, hear the word of the LORD: This is what the Sovereign LORD says: I am against the shepherds and will hold them accountable for my flock. I will remove them from tending the flock so that the shepherds can no longer feed themselves. I will rescue my flock from their mouths, and it will no longer be food for them. For this is what the Sovereign LORD says: I myself will search for my sheep and look after them. As a shep-

herd looks after his scattered flock when he is with them, so will I look after my sheep. I will rescue them from all the places where they were scattered on a day of clouds and darkness."[13]

We may seek to justify ourselves by pointing out that this was a message sent to Israel's leaders, and not to us; that the flock God was talking about was His chosen people, not the lost; and that the passage is prophetic of the Christ.

But if God has historically demonstrated his willingness to give a pink slip to poor stewards, and find another way of getting the job done, hadn't today's church best sit up and take notice? Like Israel's shepherds, we, as God's chosen, have been given "another flock" to care for as Christ's ambassadors; and like Israel's poor shepherds we are spending more time caring for ourselves than searching for our Master's flock.

The first best thing we can do for non-believing readers of Tolkien's fiction — and what I egregiously failed to do when the *Rings* coverage debuted on Hollywood Jesus — is to make it clear that Tolkien was a Christian, and that his fiction was written as an expression of his faith: "unconsciously at first, but consciously in the revision."[14] Tolkien's *Letters* and his essay "On Fairy Stories" (available in *The Tolkien Reader* in the section titled, "Tree and Leaf") provide ample, direct and irrefutable evidence of these claims, should such evidence be needed. In fact, encouraging seekers to examine these works themselves is likely to be far more effective than asking them to take someone else's word for it.

The second best thing for today's unbelieving *Rings* audience is probably a succinct explanation of Kingdom culture. Seekers need to know that those who follow Christ have in Scripture an alternative to the artificial problem of modernism (or, if you like, the artificial problem of post-modernism). The Bible does not recommend an overweening dependency on reason. "Lean not on your own understanding," says Scripture; and "do not be wise in your own eyes."[15] Neither does the Bible advocate an insensible immersion in the mystical. So we may remind seekers that Tolkien's work embraces both. "I will sing with my spirit," Tolkien's work cries, "but I will also sing with my mind."[16]

The culture of God's Kingdom, as found in His Word, is the only antidote needed to the prideful arrogance of modernity. As Paul argued on Mars Hill, there are eternal truths which the mind of man, no matter how sophisticated it may become, will never be able to grasp on its own. No matter the time period, and no matter the prevailing philosophies, God's purposes are transformational. "The Bible doesn't want to *speak to* the modern world," says William Willimon; "the Bible wants to *convert* the modern world."[17] Christianity does not offer relevance, it offers Truth; and it seeks to transform the world through a spiritual renewal of the mind.

Kingdom culture is also the antidote to the despair at the end of modernism, and cynical post-modernism. It beats the living daylights out of the thinly-veiled despair of our Fourth Age Believer, and Andreth's half-mocking hopelessness. "Desperation keeps no company with New Testament theology,"[18] says Calvin Miller. Why? Because our faith is a hope that does not disappoint; and through the evidence of God's power in His Word, in our lives and in the world around us, we may know that we have eternal life. This is a knowledge based in faith, not purely in reason. What's more, we know that love — not worldly, rational love, but love which comes as the fruit of God's Spirit — casts out fear. And our faith is not afraid to say, "Go ahead; nail me to a cross. We'll see who's right in the long run."

For some seekers, however, a more easily opened door may be a discussion of ethical morality. While certain Judeo-Christian values and a providence-dependent ethic drives the actions of Tolkien's characters, one would be ill-advised to use the moral universe of *The Lord of the Rings* as a model for guidance of personal conduct. Many readers (taking a cue from Roger Sale and company) may sense that Frodo's tactics for addressing his moral struggles and temptations are "good" within the structure of the story; and they may make the leap, in the absence of any sober critique, that the story presents a model which may bring about the same kind of success in our world. And it doesn't. This should make us uneasy.

As we have seen, Tolkien himself acknowledged that his invented world was not Christian. It provides an inadequate model of spirituality, and an inaccurate understanding of Christianity. Again, the issue is not the spirituality of Tolkien's mythology *per se*. The issue is where our Fourth Age Believer is left without saving knowledge of the Christ or the promise of the Holy Spirit.

Helping a seeker move from faith as it is found in Tolkien's world — a topic completely distinct from the nature of Tolkien's own faith — to an understanding of Christian faith will require some work. The first step may be either a presentation of the Fourth Age Believer discussion in this book, or, if a copy of *Morgoth's Ring* may be found, a review of "The Dialog of Finrod and Andreth" and Tolkien's commentary. Next would be a simple presentation of the gospel story, using perhaps Acts 2 or 1 Corinthians 15 as a guide. An illustration of the power of the Holy Spirit in the life of the believer may be presented from Galatians 5, and the contrast of the spiritual life with the worldly life can be illustrated using Romans 7 and 8. Other simple, Scripturally-based evangelism tools or catechisms may also be employed.

The importance of shepherding seekers through an understanding of *The Lord of the Rings* via Scriptural truth cannot be overemphasized. If one were led to God through Tolkien's writing, and not further taught about the saving grace of Jesus and the power of the Holy Spirit to bring healing, peace, true love and contentment — if one were merely left with the ethical monotheism of Middle-Earth — one would be left with a seriously impoverished faith indeed. The seeker may be seduced by Middle-Earth without ever being drawn to Christ.

So it may be entirely appropriate to suggest that Christians ask themselves, "What would Jesus be doing with *The Lord of the Rings* if He were me?" The answer just might be, if He were ministering to His friends on terms that would lead to the Good News, sitting in a theatre watching one of Peter Jackson's movies.

TAKING UP THE GAUNTLET

Besides the individual responsibility we shoulder to bring the lost to Christ, Tolkien's work also highlights one great shame of our present age: the seeming irrelevance of the church. To use marketing language, the challenge today's church faces "is to take those consumers who enter our churches seeking to be served and to be fed and bring them to a place where they seek — with a passion — to serve and to feed," says Deborah Windes. "The challenge is to take those who worship a god they can define and control and transform them into servants who are willing to cede their control to an almighty God."[19] Using *The Lord of the Rings* as a context for the discussion, Regina Doman eloquently describes the scope of meeting this challenge.

"I think what attracts folks to Tolkien's fiction (especially Americans) is that in some ways it is a remedy for the poisonous gas of our culture. This attraction has little to do with strictly Christian elements, although there is that in there as well. This attraction is based on, among other things: a sense of journeying and adventure, of mysterious hidden places, of profound beauty, of facing and dealing with death, of nobility, a love for a non-technological, smaller, more human economic and social order; a hatred of machines; a love of poetry and literature that isn't a 60-second sound bite; love of trees and nature.

"In a similar way, people are attracted to and fascinated with the Middle Ages and reenactments, too — why? Not necessarily because the Middle Ages were Christian, although they were. I think it's because — as a result of the Middle Ages *being* Christian — they had these attributes which flowered from the soil of their Christianity, attributes which the post-modern pagan still finds attractive because they are human: orderliness, beauty, a sense of place and position, comfortableness with earthly pleasures, love of nature, pageantry, balance, and so on.

"This is where the genius of Tolkien lies: he presents to people the flowers of Christianity — things you can only really get if you are a Christian. These flowers, ironically, are not found in the Fourth

Age beliefs of Middle-Earth. Although people have been hacking and chopping at the roots of Christianity in our culture for years, they are not humanly able to resist the sweet scent of the flowers. They don't yet understand that the flowers grew from this hated root, Christianity. The franticness of the fans of Middle-Earth is an attempt to subsist on the flowers, to preserve them and nourish themselves from them — and ultimately, the attempt is hopeless, unless they succeed (through God's grace) in tracing the flower back to its source: the Tree of Life.

"If they don't yet understand the connection between the root and the flowers — even if you point it out to them and say, 'Hey, this is all really about the Gospel!' — it is because they're just not ready yet. Their eyes are not open — no grace, or no cooperation with it.

And we can ask ourselves, is it because we Christians are not yet manifesting the flowers in our living out of the Gospel? Yes, we've got the root; isn't that interesting or seductive or sweet. But are our churches producing beautiful works of art? Are they presenting themselves as sacred and hidden places of beauty that overwhelm the senses with their glory of God? Do Christians really respect God's creation or do we senselessly accept the legacies and pride of the Industrial Revolution? Are we living a code of chivalry and nobility? Are we balanced? Is there pageantry in our churches to compete with the celebration of the fields of Cormallen?

"For the most part, in America, the answer has to be no. We don't have time. It costs too much money to do things this way. That's what liberals and New Agers do. Long hair????!!! If people can't accept the straight Gospel without all the *frou-frou*, they're not really saved.

"But that is another value of Tolkien: he shows us what we lack. If the love for Tolkien is a barometer of what is missing in our churches, then we have a lot of work to do.

"Especially because, as it should be obvious, Tolkien's book is merely a work of fiction. Tolkien never intended it to be a whole lifestyle. However, I think, the Holy Spirit, in his odd way, is using this book to show us what we need. You could say, in a way, our culture really needs Elves. And Hobbits!"[20]

Perhaps our churches do, too.

PUTTING DOWN THE BOOK

More than once, Tolkien commented on the futility of a biographical approach to artistic analysis. Whether you admire a tree or not, he said, its origin is of little significance. "The wise may know that it began with a seed, but it is vain to try and dig it up, for [the seed] no longer exists, and the virtue and powers it had now reside in the Tree."[21] If we accept Doman's analogy, the Tree is where the power always resided anyway, and Tolkien's work is only one of the many flowers on the Tree of Life. And it is time, now, for an end to analysis.

We have threshed, and hopefully we have threshed well. In our grain, perhaps, we still may find some chaff. Was it there all along, or did we track it onto the threshing floor from outside? For my part, I apologize if I have brought any in with me. "My truths may not be true, or they may be distorted: and the mirror I have made may be dim and cracked," as Tolkien said. "But I should need to be fully convinced that anything I have 'feigned' is actually harmful, *per se* and not merely because misunderstood, before I should recant or rewrite anything."[22]

Tolkien the man is above criticism because he truly consecrated his work to Christ. What about our consumption of his work? Has it been likewise consecrated? Let us strive to understand one another; and into God's hands let us all commit our spirits.

BIBLIOGRAPHY

Aeschylus. Prometheus Bound. Trans. E. H. Plumptre. Harvard Classics,
    Volume VIII, Part 4. New York: P. F. Collier & Son, 1909-14. 51
    vols. Online Edition Bartleby.com, 2001. Oct. 21, 2002,
    [www.bartleby.com/8/4/2.html].

Anderson, Laurie. "Language is a Virus." Home of the Brave. Compact Disc.
    Warner Bros., 1986.

Aquinas, Thomas. The Summa Theologica of St. Thomas Aquinas. Second
    and Revised Edition. Fathers of the English Dominican Province,
    trans. London: Burns Oates & Washbourne, 1920. 22 vols. Online
    Edition Kevin Knight, 2000. Oct. 21, 2002,
    [www.newadvent.org/summa/].

Birzer, Bradley J. J. R. R. Tolkien's Sanctifying Myth. Wilmington:
    Intercollegiate Studies Institute, 2002.

——. "The Christian Gifts of J. R. R. Tolkien." New Oxford Review 67.10
    (November 2001). Oct. 21, 2002,
    [www.newoxfordreview.org/nov01/bradleybirzer.html].

Bruner, Kurt D. Interview with Bo Emerson. "'Rings' Trilogy by Tolkien
    Blends Faith with Fantasy." The Atlanta Journal and Constitution
    Dec. 15, 2001: B.1.

Bruner, Kurt D. and Jim Ware. Finding God in The Lord of the Rings.
    Wheaton: Tyndale House Publishers, 2001.

Campbell, Joseph. The Hero With a Thousand Faces. 2nd ed. Princeton:
    Princeton University Press, 1968.

Carpenter, Humphrey. J. R. R. Tolkien: A Biography. Paperback ed.
    Boston: Houghton Mifflin, 2000.

Chesterton, G. K. The Defendant. London: J. M. Dent, 1901.

Cloud, David W. "Tolkien and The Lord Of The Rings." Logos Resource
    Pages. Logos Communication Consortium, February 5, 2002. Oct.
    21, 2002, [logosresourcepages.org/rings.htm].

Clouse, R. G. "Christian Humanism." Believe Religious Information Source.
    Oct. 21, 2002, [mb-soft.com/believe/txn/chrishum.htm].

Cowper, William. Hymns of the Christian Church. Ed. Charles W. Eliot.
    Harvard Classics, Volume XLV, Part 2. New York: P. F. Collier &
    Son, 1909-14. 51 vols. Online Edition Bartleby.com, 2001. Oct.
    21, 2002, [www.bartleby.com/45/2.html].

Curry, Patrick. Defending Middle-Earth: Tolkien, Myth and Modernity.
    Houndmills, Basingstoke: Palgrave Macmillan, 1997.

Doman, Regina. [regina@veraprise.com]. "RE: Next Installment." Private e-
    mail message to Greg Wright, [hjlotr@hotmail.com]. April 2, 2002.

——. [regina@schmiedicke.com]. "RE: Tolkien Knew: No Salvation in
    Hobbits." Private e-mail message to Greg Wright,
    [hjlotr@hotmail.com]. February 26, 2002.

——. [regina@veraprise.com]. "RE: Your Help, Please." Private e-mail message to Greg Wright, [hjlotr@hotmail.com]. June 20, 2002.

Education of Max Bickford, The. "Revisionism." Dir. David Platt. Perf.
Richard Dreyfuss, Marcia Gay Harden, Helen Shaver, Regina Taylor,
Katee Sackhoff, Eric Ian Goldberg, Karen Kandel. November 18,
2001. CBS.

Emerson, Ralph Waldo. The Complete Works of Ralph Waldo Emerson.
Centenary Edition. 12 vols. Boston & New York: Houghton Mifflin
and Company, 1903-1904.

Foster, Robert. The Complete Guide to Middle-Earth. New York: Ballantine
Books, 1978.

Fox, James J. "Natural Law." The Catholic Encyclopedia. Volume 9. New
York: Robert Appleton Company, 1910. 15 vols. Online Edition:
Kevin Knight, 1999. Oct. 21, 2002,
[www.newadvent.org/cathen/09076a.htm].

Fuller, Edmund. "The Lord of the Hobbits." Ed. Issacs and Zimbardo.
Tolkien and the Critics. Notre Dame: University of Notre Dame
Press, 1968. Pages 17-39.

George, Timothy. "Providence." Holman Bible Dictionary for Windows.
Version 1.0g. Parsons Technology, 1994.

"Heidelberg Catechism." The Internet Sacred Text Archive. J. B. Hare, 1997-
2001. Oct. 21, 2002, [www.sacred-texts.com/chr/heidcat.htm].

Herodotus. The Histories. Ed. George Rawlinson. Great Books of the
Western World. Volume 6. Chicago: Encyclopedia Brittanica, 1952.
54 vols.

Hibbs, Thomas S. "Popes, Philosophers and Peeping Thomists." Christian
History 21.1 (Issue 73, Winter 2002). Pages 40-42.

Holy Bible. King James Version (KJV). Electronic Edition. Quickverse for
Windows 3.0d. Craig Rairdin and Parsons Technology Inc., 1992-
1994.

Holy Bible. New American Standard Version (NASB). The Lockman
Foundation, 1960-1988. Electronic Edition. Quickverse for
Windows 3.0d. Craig Rairdin and Parsons Technology Inc., 1992-
1994.

Isaacs, Neil D., and Rose A. Zimbardo, eds. Tolkien and the Critics. Notre
Dame: University of Notre Dame Press, 1968.

Kemerling, Garth. "Humanism." A Dictionary of Philosophical Terms and
Names. Philosophy Pages, 1997-2002. Oct. 21, 2002, [www.philos-
ophypages.com/dy/h9.htm#huma].

——. "Just War Theory." A Dictionary of Philosophical Terms and Names.
Philosophy Pages, 1997-2002. Nov. 7, 2002, [www.philosophy-
pages.com/dy/j.htm#jusw].

——. "Post-modernism." A Dictionary of Philosophical Terms and Names.
Philosophy Pages, 1997-2002. Oct. 21, 2002, [www.philosophy-
pages.com/dy/p7.htm#pomo].

Knight, Gareth. The Magical World of J. R. R. Tolkien. Oceanside: Sun
Chalice Books, 2001.

Kohl, Benjamin G. "Humanism." Believe Religious Information Source.
    Oct. 21, 2002, [mb-soft.com/believe/txn/chrishum.htm].
Lee, H. Page. "Consecration." Holman Bible Dictionary for Windows.
    Version 1.0g. Parsons Technology, 1994.
Lewis, C. S. "The Dethronement of Power." Ed. Issacs and Zimbardo.
    Tolkien and the Critics. Notre Dame: University of Notre Dame
    Press, 1968. Pages 12-16.
Lucas, George. Interview with Bill Moyers. "Of Myth and Men." Time
    Magazine April 26, 1999. June 16, 2002, [www.time.com].
Mayberry, Susanah. My Amiable Uncle: Recollections About Booth
    Tarkington. West Lafayette: Purdue University Press, 1983.
Miller, Calvin. The Empowered Communicator. Nashville: Broadman &
    Holman, 1994.
O'Connor, Flannery. Letters of Flannery O'Connor: The Habit of Being. Ed.
    Sally Fitzgerald. New York: Farrar, Straus & Giroux, 1979.
Ortiz, Juan Carlos. Disciple. Lake Mary: Creation House, 1995.
Owen, Wilfred. The Collected Poems of Wilfred Owen. Ed. C. Day Lewis.
    New York: New Directions Publishing Company, 1963.
Patten, Wesley. Sermon. "God Will Speak to Us Through His Word."
    Normandy Christian Church, May 23,1993.
Pearce, Joseph. Interview. "J. R. R. Tolkien's Take on the Truth." Zenit - The
    World Seen From Rome November 15, 2001. Oct. 21, 2002,
    [zenit.org/english].
Pearce, Joseph. Tolkien: Man and Myth. San Francisco: Ignatius Press, 2001.
Pearce, Joseph. "True Myth: The Catholicism of The Lord of the Rings".
    Catholic World Report Dossier 11.11 (December 2001). Oct. 21
    2002, [www.catholic.net/RCC/Periodicals/Igpress/2001-
    12/dossier.html].
Reilly, Robert J. "Tolkien and the Fairy Story." Ed. Issacs and Zimbardo.
    Tolkien and the Critics. Notre Dame: University of Notre Dame
    Press, 1968. Pages 128-150.
Robbins, Vernon K. "Salvation History." Dictionary of Socio-Rhetorical
    Terms. Emory University, 1999. Oct. 21, 2002,
    [www.emory.edu/COLLEGE/RELIGION/faculty/robbins/SRI/defns/
    s_defns.html].
Russ, Joanna. Lecture. University of Washington, April 1984.
Sale, Roger. "Tolkien and Frodo Baggins." Ed. Issacs and Zimbardo.
    Tolkien and the Critics. Notre Dame: University of Notre Dame
    Press, 1968. Pages 247-288.
Shippey, Tom. Interview with Claire E. White. "Talking Tolkien with
    Thomas Shippey." The Internet Writing Journal 6.2 (March 2002).
    Oct. 28, 2002, [www.writerswrite.com/journal/mar02/shippey.htm].
Shippey, Tom. Lecture. "Tolkien and Iceland: The Philology of Envy." The
    University of Iceland, Reykjavik. September 13, 2002.
Smith, Mark Eddy. Tolkien's Ordinary Virtues: Exploring the Spiritual
    Themes of the Lord of the Rings. Downers Grove: Intervarsity

Press, 2002.

Snider, P. Joel. "Gospel." Holman Bible Dictionary for Windows. Version
    1.0g. Parsons Technology, 1994.

Sugrue, Michael. Lecture. "Introduction to the Problems and Scope of
    Philosophy." The Great Minds of the Western Intellectual Tradition.
    Vol. 1. 2nd ed. Videocassette. Springfield: The Teaching Company
    Limited Partnership, 1995. 6 vols.

———. Lecture. "Pascal's *Pensées*." The Great Minds of the Western
    Intellectual Tradition. Vol. 2. 2nd ed. Videocassette. Springfield:
    The Teaching Company Limited Partnership, 1995. 6 vols.

Tarkington, Booth. "The Fascinating Stranger" and Other Stories. New York:
    Doubleday, Page & Company, 1923.

———. Dr. Panofsky and Mr. Tarkington: An Exchange of Letters, 1938-1946.
    Ed. Richard M. Ludwig. Princeton: Princeton University Library,
    1974.

———. Growth. New York: Doubleday, Page & Company, 1927.

———. Kate Fennigate. New York: Doubleday, Doran & Company, 1943.

———. Some Old Portraits. New York: Doubleday, Doran & Company, 1939.

Thoreau, Henry David. "Economy." Walden. The Thoreau Reader. Richard
    Lenat, 2001-2002. Nov. 18, 2002,
    [eserver.org/thoreau/walden1a.html].

Tolkien, Christopher. Foreword. Morgoth's Ring: The Later Silmarillion, Part
    One. J. R. R. Tolkien. The History of Middle-Earth. Vol. 10.
    Boston & New York: Houghton Mifflin Company, 1993. 12 vols.

Tolkien, J. R. R. The Fellowship of the Ring. 2nd ed. Boston: Houghton
    Mifflin Company, 1965.

———. Letters. Ed. Humphrey Carpenter. Boston & New York: Houghton
    Mifflin Company, 2000.

———. Morgoth's Ring: The Later Silmarillion, Part One. Ed. Christopher
    Tolkien. The History of Middle-Earth. Vol. 10. Boston & New
    York: Houghton Mifflin Company, 1993. 12 vols.

———. The Return of the King. 2nd ed. Boston: Houghton Mifflin Company,
    1965.

———. The Return of the Shadow: The History of the Lord of the Rings, Volume
    1. Ed. Christopher Tolkien. The History of Middle-Earth. Vol. 6.
    Boston & New York: Houghton Mifflin Company, 1988. 12 vols.

———. The Silmarillion. Ed. Christopher Tolkien. Boston: Houghton Mifflin
    Company, 1977.

———. The Tolkien Reader. New York: Ballantine Books, 1966.

———. The Two Towers. 2nd ed. Boston: Houghton Mifflin Company, 1965.

———. Unfinished Tales. Ed. Christopher Tolkien. Boston: Houghton Mifflin
    Company, 1980.

Traylor, John H., Jr. "Chronicles, Books of." Holman Bible Dictionary for
    Windows. Version 1.0g. Parsons Technology, 1994.

Untouchables, The. Dir. Brian de Palma. Perf. Kevin Costner, Charles Martin
    Smith, Andy Garcia, Robert deNiro, Sean Connery. 1987.

Videocassette. Paramount, 1988.

Webster's New World Dictionary of the American Language, Second College
  Edition. New York: Simon & Schuster, 1984.

Whalley, George. The Legend of John Hornby. Toronto: Macmillan of
  Canada, 1962.

Wiersbe, Warren. Preaching and Teaching with Imagination: The Quest for
  Biblical Ministry. Wheaton: Victor Books - SP Publications, 1994.

Willimon, William H. "This Culture is Overrated." Leadership Journal 18.1
  (Winter 1997). Page 29.

Windes, Deborah. "The Cost of Living in a Suburban Paradise." Books and
  Culture 4.1 (January/February 1998). Page 6.

Woodress, James. Booth Tarkington, Gentleman from Indiana. Philadelphia
  & New York: Lippincott, 1955.

Yeats, William Butler. Epigraph. Responsibilities. The Columbia World of
  Quotations. New York: Columbia University Press, 1996. Oct. 21,
  2002, [www.bartleby.com/66/].

Zinneman, Fred. Interview with Brian Neve. "Fred Zinneman: A Past Master
  of His Craft." Cineaste 23.1 (1997). Pages 15-19.

NOTES

PREFACE

1. Booth Tarkington in Susanah Mayberry, My Amiable Uncle:
    Recollections About Booth Tarkington (West Lafayette: Purdue
    University Press, 1983), p. 88.

2. Joseph Pearce, "True Myth: The Catholicism of *The Lord of the Rings*"
    (Catholic World Report Dossier 11.11, December 2001) Oct. 21 2002
    [www.catholic.net/RCC/Periodicals/Igpress/2001-12/dossier.html].

3. J. R. R. Tolkien, Letters (Boston & New York: Houghton Mifflin
    Company, 2000), no. 123, to Milton Waldman, 1950.

CHAPTER ONE: MYTH, CULTURE AND CONSECRATION

1. The Education of Max Bickford, "Revisionism" Dir. David Platt, Perf.
    Richard Dreyfuss, Marcia Gay Harden, Helen Shaver, Regina Taylor,
    Katee Sackhoff, Eric Ian Goldberg, Karen Kandel (CBS, November 18,
    2001).

2. George Whalley, The Legend of John Hornby (Toronto: Macmillan of
    Canada, 1962), p. 130.

3. C. Day Lewis in Wilfred Owen, The Collected Poems of Wilfred Owen
    Ed. C. Day Lewis (New York: New Directions Publishing Company,
    1963), p. 17.

4. Wilfred Own, op. cit., p. 42.

5. J. R. R. Tolkien, Letters, op. cit., no. 66, to Christopher Tolkien, 1944.

6. Ibid., no. 96, to Christopher Tolkien, 1945.

7. Ibid., no. 131, to Milton Waldman, 1951.

8. Herodotus, The Histories Ed. George Rawlinson Great Books of the Western World Volume 6 (Chicago: Encyclopedia Brittanica, 1952), 3.102-105.

9. "Myth," Webster's New World Dictionary of the American Language Second College Edition (New York: Simon & Schuster, 1984).

10. "Ostensible," Webster's, op. cit.

11. Leviticus 23:42-43.

12. Deuteronomy 10:19.

13. Deuteronomy 16:1-3.

14. Deuteronomy 31:9-13.

15. Judges 21:25.

16. Deuteronomy 17:16-18.

17. John H. Traylor, Jr., "Chronicles, Books of" Holman Bible Dictionary for Windows Version 1.0g (Parsons Technology, 1994).

18. Romans 11:1-8.

19. 1 Peter 2:9-10.

20. 1 Peter 2:5.

21. John 20:30-31.

22. John 1:12-13.

23. Luke 1:3.

24. P. Joel Snider, "Gospel" Holman Bible Dictionary for Windows Version 1.0g (Parsons Technology, 1994).

25. J. R. R. Tolkien, Letters, op. cit., no. 89, to Christopher Tolkien, 1944.

26. J. R. R. Tolkien, The Tolkien Reader (New York: Ballantine Books, 1966) p. 75.

27. Mark 9: 39-40.

28. Matthew 12:30.

29. 1 Timothy 4:4-6.

30. Matthew 23:19.

31. H. Page Lee, "Consecration" Holman Bible Dictionary for Windows Version 1.0g (Parsons Technology, 1994).

32. Booth Tarkington, Dr. Panofsky and Mr. Tarkington: An Exchange of Letters, 1938-1946 Ed. Richard M. Ludwig (Princeton: Princeton University Library, 1974) p. 72.

33. George Lucas, Interview with Bill Moyers "Of Myth and Men" (Time Magazine April 26, 1999) §29. June 16, 2002 [www.time.com].

34. Joseph Campbell, The Hero With a Thousand Faces 2nd ed. (Princeton: Princeton University Press, 1968), p. 30.

35. Regina Doman [regina@veraprise.com], "RE: Next Installment" (Private e-mail message to Greg Wright [hjlotr@hotmail.com], 2 April 2002).

36. Michael Sugrue, Lecture "Introduction to the Problems and Scope of Philosophy" The Great Minds of the Western Intellectual Tradition Vol. 1 2nd ed. Videocassette (Springfield: The Teaching Company Limited Partnership, 1995).

37. Michael Sugrue, Lecture "Pascal's *Pensées*" The Great Minds of the Western Intellectual Tradition Vol. 2 2nd ed. Videocassette (Springfield: The Teaching Company Limited Partnership, 1995).

38. George Lucas, op. cit., §18.

39. Ibid., §15.

40. John 3:7.

41. John 4:14.

42. George Lucas, op. cit., §25.

43. John 4:15.

44. George Lucas, op. cit., §15.

45. Ibid., §13.

46. Ibid., §9.

CHAPTER TWO: A FANTASTIC MYTHOLOGY

1. C.S. Lewis, "The Dethronement of Power" Ed. Issacs and Zimbardo Tolkien and the Critics (Notre Dame: University of Notre Dame Press, 1968), p. 15.

2. Ibid.

3. Joseph Campbell, op. cit., p. 3.

4. J. R. R. Tolkien, Letters, op. cit., no. 163, to W. H. Auden, 1955.

5. Ibid., footnote to no. 131, to Milton Waldman, 1951.

6. Ibid., no. 4, To Edith Bratt, 1916.

7. J. R. R. Tolkien, The Tolkien Reader, op. cit., p. 65.

8. J. R. R. Tolkien, Letters, op. cit., no. 257, to Christopher Bretherton, 1964.

9. J. R. R. Tolkien, The Return of the Shadow: The History of the Lord of the Rings, Volume 1 Ed. Christopher Tolkien The History of Middle-Earth Vol. 6 (Boston & New York: Houghton Mifflin Company, 1988),

p.7.

10. J. R. R. Tolkien, Letters, op. cit., no. 19, to Stanley Unwin, 1937.
11. Ibid., no. 131, to Milton Waldman, 1951.
12. Joanna Russ, Lecture (University of Washington, April 1984).
13. Joseph Campbell, op. cit., p. 30.
14. J. R. R. Tolkien, Unfinished Tales Ed. Christopher Tolkien (Boston: Houghton Mifflin Company, 1980), p. 2.
15. Christopher Tolkien in J. R. R. Tolkien, The Silmarillion Ed. Christopher Tolkien (Boston: Houghton Mifflin Company, 1977), p.7.
16. Christopher Tolkien in J. R. R. Tolkien, Unfinished Tales, op. cit., p. 1.
17. Ibid, p. 1f.
18. J. R. R. Tolkien, Morgoth's Ring: The Later Silmarillion, Part One Ed. Christopher Tolkien The History of Middle-Earth Vol. 10 (Boston & New York: Houghton Mifflin Company, 1993), p. 342.
19. J. R. R. Tolkien, The Fellowship of the Ring 2nd ed. (Boston: Houghton Mifflin Company, 1965), p. 24.
20. J. R. R. Tolkien, The Return of the King 2nd ed. (Boston: Houghton Mifflin Company, 1965), p. 411ff.
21. Christopher Tolkien in J. R. R. Tolkien, The Silmarillion, op. cit., p. 8.
22. The paragraphs which follow are a summary of material from "Ainulindale" and "Valaquenta" in J. R. R. Tolkien, The Silmarillion, op. cit., pp. 13-34.
23. J. R. R. Tolkien, Morgoth's Ring, op. cit., p. 330.
24. Tom Shippey, Lecture "Tolkien and Iceland: The Philology of Envy" (The University of Iceland, Reykjavik, September 13, 2002).
25. J. R. R. Tolkien, Letters, op. cit., no. 131, to Milton Waldman, 1951.
26. J. R. R. Tolkien, The Fellowship of the Ring, op. cit., p. 11.
27. J. R. R. Tolkien, The Return of the King, op. cit., p. 344.
28. Ibid, p. 308.
29. J. R. R. Tolkien, The Fellowship of the Ring, op. cit., p. 10.
30. Robert Foster, The Complete Guide to Middle-Earth (New York: Ballantine Books, 1978) p. ix.
31. J. R. R. Tolkien, Letters, op. cit., no. 131, to Milton Waldman, 1951.

CHAPTER THREE: TOLKIEN AND MODERNITY

1. Laurie Anderson, "Language is a Virus" Home of the Brave Compact Disc (Warner Bros., 1986).
2. Aeschylus, Prometheus Bound Trans. E. H. Plumptre Harvard Classics

Volume VIII:4 (New York: P. F. Collier & Son, 1909-14; Online Edition Bartleby.com, 2001). Oct. 21, 2002, [www.bartleby.com/8/4/2.html].

3. Mark 8:36.

4. 1 Corithians 13:12.

5. Garth Kemerling, "Post-modernism" A Dictionary of Philosophical Terms and Names (Philosophy Pages, 1997-2002). Oct. 21, 2002 [www.philosophypages.com/dy/p7.htm#pomo].

6. Booth Tarkington, Kate Fennigate (New York: Doubleday, Doran & Company, 1943), p. 128.

7. Booth Tarkington, "The Fascinating Stranger" and Other Stories (New York: Doubleday, Page & Company, 1923), p. 368f.

8. Booth Tarkington, Growth (New York: Doubleday, Page & Company, 1927), p. 1.

9. J. R. R. Tolkien, Letters, op. cit., no. 19, to Stanley Unwin, 1937.

10. J. R. R. Tolkien, The Tolkien Reader, op. cit., p. 83.

11. Booth Tarkington, "The Fascinating Stranger" and Other Stories, op. cit., pp. 363ff.

12. J. R. R. Tolkien, Letters, op. cit., no. 73, to Christopher Tolkien, 1944.

13. Ibid., no. 53, to Christopher Tolkien, 1943.

14. Robert J. Reilly, "Tolkien and the Fairy Story" Ed. Issacs and Zimbardo Tolkien and the Critics (Notre Dame: University of Notre Dame Press, 1968), p. 130.

15. Ibid., p. 129.

16. Christopher Tolkien in J. R. R. Tolkien, Morgoth's Ring, op. cit., p. 371.

17. Booth Tarkington quoted in James Woodress, Booth Tarkington, Gentleman from Indiana (Philadelphia & New York: Lippincott, 1955), p. 207.

18. Robert J. Reilly, op. cit., p. 137.

19. Roger Sale, "Tolkien and Frodo Baggins" Ed. Issacs and Zimbardo Tolkien and the Critics (Notre Dame: University of Notre Dame Press, 1968), p. 247.

20. Joseph Campbell, op. cit., p. 390f.

21. Ibid., p. 391.

22. Roger Sale, op. cit., p. 288.

23. J. R. R. Tolkien, Letters, op. cit., no. 76, to Christopher Tolkien, 1944.

24. Ibid., no. 131, to Milton Waldman, 1951.

25. Ibid., no. 309, to Amy Ronald, 1969.

26. Ibid., no. 200, to Major R. Bowen, 1957.

27. Christopher Tolkien in J. R. R. Tolkien, <u>Morgoth's Ring</u>, op. cit., p. 371.
28. J. R. R. Tolkien, <u>Morgoth's Ring</u>, op. cit., p. 378.
29. J. R. R. Tolkien, <u>Letters</u>, op. cit., footnote to no. 131, to Milton Waldman, 1951.
30. J. R. R. Tolkien, <u>Morgoth's Ring</u>, op. cit., p. 370.
31. Christopher Tolkien in J. R. R. Tolkien, <u>Morgoth's Ring</u>, op. cit., p. 371.
32. J. R. R. Tolkien, <u>Letters</u>, op. cit., no. 181, to Michael Straight, 1956.
33. J. R. R. Tolkien, <u>The Tolkien Reader</u>, op. cit., p. 75.
34. J. R. R. Tolkien, <u>Morgoth's Ring</u>, op. cit., p. 370.
35. Ibid.
36. William Butler Yeats, Epigraph <u>Responsibilities</u> <u>The Columbia World of Quotations</u> (New York: Columbia University Press, 1996). Oct. 21, 2002 [www.bartleby.com/66/].

CHAPTER FOUR: TOLKIEN'S FAITH

1. Flannery O'Connor, <u>Letters of Flannery O'Connor: The Habit of Being</u> Ed. Sally Fitzgerald (New York: Farrar, Straus & Giroux, 1979), p. 143.
2. Flannery O'Connor, paraphrased in Thomas S. Hibbs, "Popes, Philosophers and Peeping Thomists" (<u>Christian History</u> 21.1, Issue 73, Winter 2002), p. 42.
3. Acts 17:11.
4. Wesley Patten, Sermon "God Will Speak to Us Through His Word" (Normandy Christian Church, May 23,1993).
5. James 4:8, NASB.
6. Sean Connery in <u>The Untouchables</u> Dir. Brian de Palma, Perf. Kevin Costner, Charles Martin Smith, Andy Garcia, Robert deNiro, Sean Connery 1987 Videocassette (Paramount, 1988).
7. J. R. R. Tolkien, <u>Letters</u>, op. cit., no. 269, to W. H. Auden, 1965.
8. Ibid., no. 131, to Milton Waldman, 1951.
9. Ibid., no. 66, to Christopher Tolkien, 1944.
10. Ibid., no. 155, to Naomi Mitchison, 1954.
11. J. R. R. Tolkien, <u>Unfinished Tales</u>, footnote 3 on p. 401.
12. J. R. R. Tolkien, <u>The Two Towers</u> 2nd ed. (Boston: Houghton Mifflin Company, 1965), p. 329.
13. J. R. R. Tolkien, <u>Letters</u>, op. cit., no. 156, to Robert Murray, 1954.
14. Ibid., no. 211, to Rhona Beare, 1958.
15. J. R. R. Tolkien, <u>The Tolkien Reader</u>, op. cit., p. 39.
16. J. R. R. Tolkien, <u>The Return of the Shadow</u>, op. cit., p. 215.

17. J. R. R. Tolkien, The Tolkien Reader, op. cit., p. 55.
18. J. R. R. Tolkien, Morgoth's Ring, op. cit., p. 144.
19. Ibid., p.15.
20. J. R. R. Tolkien, The Return of the Shadow, op. cit., p. 182.
21. Christopher Tolkien in J. R. R. Tolkien, Morgoth's Ring, op. cit., p. 372, quoting from The Book of Lost Tales.
22. J. R. R. Tolkien, Morgoth's Ring, op. cit., p. 330.
23. "Archangel," Webster's, op. cit.
24. J. R. R. Tolkien, Morgoth's Ring, op. cit., p. 147.
25. J. R. R. Tolkien, Letters, op. cit., no. 89, to Christopher Tolkien, 1944.
26. Ibid., footnote to no. 181, to Michael Straight, 1956.
27. Genesis 6:4.
28. Regina Doman [regina@schmiedicke.com], "RE: Tolkien Knew: No Salvation in Hobbits" (Private e-mail message to Greg Wright, [hjlotr@hotmail.com] 26 February 2002).
29. J. R. R. Tolkien, Letters, footnote to no. 181, to Michael Straight, 1956.
30. Regina Doman, "RE: Next Installment," op. cit.
31. Ibid.
32. J. R. R. Tolkien, Letters, op. cit., no. 131, to Milton Waldman, 1951.
33. J. R. R. Tolkien, The Tolkien Reader, op. cit., p. 51.
34. J. R. R. Tolkien, Morgoth's Ring, op. cit., p. 336.
35. Ibid., p. 377.
36. J. R. R. Tolkien, Letters, op. cit., no. 131, to Milton Waldman, 1951.
37. Attributed to William Faulkner in Fred Zinneman, Interview with Brian Neve "Fred Zinneman: A Past Master of His Craft" (Cineaste 23.1, 1997), p.19.
38. J. R. R. Tolkien, Letters, op. cit., no. 5, to Geoffrey B. Smith, 1916.
39. Ibid., no. 63, to Christopher Tolkien, 1944.
40. Ibid., no. 310, to Camilla Unwin, 1969.
41. J. R. R. Tolkien, The Tolkien Reader, op. cit., p. 89.
42. Ibid., p. 48f.
43. Ibid., p. 60.
44. Ibid., p. 70.
45. Ibid., p. 71.
46. J. R. R. Tolkien, Letters, op. cit., no. 93, to Christopher Tolkien, 1944.
47. J. R. R. Tolkien, The Tolkien Reader, op. cit., p. 77.
48. Philippians 4:8.
49. J. R. R. Tolkien, The Tolkien Reader, op. cit., p. 86.

50. Ibid., p. 85.
51. Ibid., p. 63.
52. Ibid., p. 74.
53. Ibid., p. 89.
54. Ibid.
55. Ibid, p. 88.
56. J. R. R. Tolkien, Letters, op. cit., no. 43, to Michael Tolkien, 1941.
57. Regina Doman, "RE: Next Installment," op. cit.
58. J. R. R. Tolkien, Letters, op. cit., no. 142, to Robert Murray, 1953.
59. Christopher Tolkien in J. R. R. Tolkien, The Return of the Shadow, op. cit., p. 280.
60. J. R. R. Tolkien, The Return of the King, op. cit., p. 191.
61. J. R. R. Tolkien, Letters, op. cit., no. 153, to Peter Hastings, 1954.
62. Ibid., no. 213, to Deborah Webster, 1958.
63. Ibid., no. 87, to Christopher Tolkien, 1944.
64. J. R. R. Tolkien, Morgoth's Ring, op. cit., p. 308f.
65. Ibid., p. 315.
66. Ibid., p. 310.
67. J. R. R. Tolkien, Letters, op. cit., no. 75, to Chistopher Tolkien, 1944.
68. J. R. R. Tolkien, Morgoth's Ring, op. cit., footnote on p. 392.
69. Matthew 19:17.
70. J. R. R. Tolkien, Morgoth's Ring, op. cit., p. 21.
71. J. R. R. Tolkien, Letters, op. cit., no. 43, to Michael Tolkien, 1941.
72. Ibid., no. 69, to Christopher Tolkien, 1944.
73. Ibid., no. 131, to Milton Waldman, 1951.
74. Ibid.
75. Ibid., no 181, to Michael Straight, 1956.
76. Ibid., no. 192, to Amy Ronald, 1956.
77. Ibid., no. 191, to Miss J. Burn, 1956.
78. Ibid., footnote to no. 246, to Eileen Elgar, 1963.
79. Ibid., no. 96, to Christopher Tolkien, 1945.
80. Ibid.
81. Booth Tarkington, quoted in James Woodress, op. cit., p. 303.
82. J. R. R. Tolkien, Morgoth's Ring, op. cit., p. 314.
83. Ibid., p. 307.
84. Ibid., p. 317.
85. Ibid., p. 320.

86. J. R. R. Tolkien, <u>Letters</u>, op. cit., no. 181, to Michael Straight, 1956.

87. J. R. R. Tolkien, <u>Morgoth's Ring</u>, op. cit., p. 320.

88. Ibid., p. 338.

89. J. R. R. Tolkien, <u>Letters</u>, op. cit., no. 89, to Christopher Tolkien, 1944.

90. Ibid., no. 45, to Michael Tolkien, 1941.

91. J. R. R. Tolkien, <u>Morgoth's Ring</u>, op. cit., p. 21.

92. Ibid., p. 9.

93. See 1 Corinthians 13:12.

94. J. R. R. Tolkien, <u>Morgoth's Ring</u>, op. cit., p. 321.

95. J. R. R. Tolkien, <u>Letters</u>, op. cit., no. 54, to Christopher Tolkien, 1944.

96. Ibid., no. 246, to Eileen Elgar, 1963.

97. Ibid., no. 96, to Christopher Tolkien, 1945.

98. Ibid., no. 123, to Milton Waldman, 1950.

99. Ibid., no. 195, to Amy Ronald, 1956.

100. C. S. Lewis, op. cit., p. 15.

CHAPTER FIVE: A CONSECRATED *LORD OF THE RINGS*

1. J. R. R. Tolkien, <u>Letters</u>, op. cit., no. 109, to Stanley Unwin, 1947.

2. Ibid., no. 181, to Michael Straight, 1956.

3. J. R. R. Tolkien, <u>The Fellowship of the Ring</u>, op. cit., p. 182.

4. J. R. R. Tolkien, <u>The Return of the King</u>, op. cit., p. 136.

5. J. R. R. Tolkien, <u>The Two Towers</u>, op. cit., p. 311.

6. Luke 12:42-43, KJV.

7. J. R. R. Tolkien, <u>The Fellowship of the Ring</u>, op. cit., p. 341.

8. J. R. R. Tolkien, <u>The Two Towers</u>, op. cit., p. 98.

9. Ibid., p. 106.

10. Ibid., p.103.

11. Ibid., p.104.

12. J. R. R. Tolkien, <u>The Fellowship of the Ring</u>, op. cit., p. 413.

13. Hebrews 4:15.

14. Matthew 7:13-14.

15. J. R. R. Tolkien, <u>The Fellowship of the Ring</u>, op. cit., p. 292.

16. Ibid., p. 53.

17. Ibid., p. 52.

18. Matthew 24:6.

19. J. R. R. Tolkien, <u>The Fellowship of the Ring</u>, op. cit., p. 363.

20. John 1:5.

21. Timothy George, "Providence" <u>Holman Bible Dictionary for Windows</u>

Version 1.0g (Parsons Technology, 1994).

22. "Heidelberg Catechism," The Internet Sacred Text Archive (J. B. Hare, 1997-2001). 21 Oct. 2002 [www.sacred-texts.com/chr/heidcat.htm].

23. J. R. R. Tolkien, The Fellowship of the Ring, op. cit., p. 65.

24. Ibid., p. 70.

25. Ibid., p. 94.

26. Ibid., p. 253.

27. Ibid., p. 284.

28. Proverbs 19:21.

29. Ephesians 2:10.

30. J. R. R. Tolkien, The Return of the King, op. cit., p. 129.

31. Ibid., p. 116.

32. William Cowper, Hymns of the Christian Church Ed. Charles W. Eliot Harvard Classics Volume XLV:2 (New York: P. F. Collier & Son, 1909-14, Online Edition Bartleby.com, 2001). 21 Oct. 2002 [www.bartleby.com/45/2.html].

33. J. R. R. Tolkien, Letters, op. cit., no. 131, to Milton Waldman, 1951.

34. Juan Carlos Ortiz, Disciple (Lake Mary: Creation House, 1995), p. 63.

35. J. R. R. Tolkien, The Return of the King, op. cit., p. 57.

36. J. R. R. Tolkien, The Two Towers, op. cit., p. 38.

37. Ibid., p. 144.

38. 1 Corinthians 7:29.

39. J. R. R. Tolkien, The Fellowship of the Ring, op. cit., p. 60.

40. J. R. R. Tolkien, The Two Towers, op. cit., p. 231.

41. John 15:13.

42. J. R. R. Tolkien, The Return of the King, op. cit., p. 341.

43. Romans 5:3-4.

44. J. R. R. Tolkien, The Two Towers, op. cit., p. 321.

45. Hebrews 10:36.

46. Isaiah 40:31.

47. Romans 1:17.

48. Hebrews 10:39.

49. J. R. R. Tolkien, The Two Towers, op. cit., p. 321.

50. Acts 13:36.

51. J. R. R. Tolkien, The Fellowship of the Ring, op. cit., p. 69.

52. J. R. R. Tolkien, The Two Towers, op. cit., p. 221.

53. James 2:13.

54. J. R. R. Tolkien, Letters, op. cit., footnote to No. 153, to Peter Hastings,

1954.

55. J. R. R. Tolkien, The Two Towers, op. cit., p. 124.
56. Ibid., p. 160.
57. J. R. R. Tolkien, The Fellowship of the Ring, op. cit., p. 362.
58. 1 John 2:10-11.
59. J. R. R. Tolkien, The Fellowship of the Ring, op. cit., p. 371.
60. Matthew 5:44.
61. 1 Corinthians 13:5.
62. Mark 3:26.
63. J. R. R. Tolkien, The Fellowship of the Ring, op. cit., p. 381.
64. Ibid., p. 384.
65. Ibid., p. 373.
66. Ibid.
67. James 1:14.
68. J. R. R. Tolkien, The Fellowship of the Ring, op. cit., p. 414.
69. Ibid., p. 412.
70. J. R. R. Tolkien, The Two Towers, op. cit., p. 204.
71. J. R. R. Tolkien, Letters, op. cit., no. 131, to Milton Waldman, 1951.
72. J. R. R. Tolkien, The Return of the King, op. cit., p. 154.
73. Ibid., p. 155.
74. J. R. R. Tolkien, Letters, op. cit., no. 17, to Stanley Unwin, 1937.
75. Ibid., no. 52, to Christopher Tolkien, 1943.
76. Ibid., no. 159, to Dora Marshall, 1955.
77. Ibid., no. 64, to Christopher Tolkien, 1944.
78. J. R. R. Tolkien, The Tolkien Reader, op. cit., p. 86.
79. J. R. R. Tolkien, The Return of the King, op. cit., p. 275.
80. John 13:33-14:20, NASB.

CHAPTER SIX: TOLKIEN'S "FOURTH AGE"

1. Christopher Tolkien, "Foreword," Morgoth's Ring, op. cit., p. vii.
2. J. R. R. Tolkien, Letters, op. cit., no. 163, to W.H. Auden, 1955.
3. Christopher Tolkien in J. R. R. Tolkien, Morgoth's Ring, op. cit., p. 369.
4. Ibid.
5. Humphrey Carpenter, J. R. R. Tolkien: A Biography Paperback ed. (Boston: Houghton Mifflin, 2000), p. 252.
6. Ibid., p. 241.
7. J. R. R. Tolkien, Letters, op. cit., no. 169, to Hugh Brogan, 1955.
8. J. R. R. Tolkien, The Return of the Shadow, op. cit., p. 41.

9. J. R. R. Tolkien, Letters, op. cit., no. 294, to Charlotte and Denis Plimmer, 1967.
10. Ibid., no. 165, to Houghton Mifflin, 1955.
11. Ibid., no. 257, to Christopher Bretherton, 1964.
12. Ibid., no. 131, to Milton Waldman, 1951.
13. Ibid., no. 156, to Robert Murray, 1954.
14. Ibid., no. 211, to Rhona Beare, 1958.
15. J. R. R. Tolkien, Morgoth's Ring, op. cit., p. 5, c. 1948, from draft of letter to Mrs. Farrar (Letter No. 115).
16. Ibid.
17. Ibid.
18. J. R. R. Tolkien, Letters, op. cit., no. 186, to Joanna de Bortadano, 1956.
19. Ibid., no. 211, to Rhona Beare, 1958.
20. Ibid., no. 122, to Naomi Mitchison, 1949.
21. Christopher Tolkien in J. R. R. Tolkien, Morgoth's Ring, op. cit., p. 281, referencing as an example the ride of Oromë from Aman to Middle-Earth.
22. J. R. R. Tolkien, Letters, op. cit., no. 154, to Naomi Mitchison, 1954.
23. J. R. R. Tolkien, Morgoth's Ring, op. cit., p. 338.
24. Ibid., p. 420.
25. J. R. R. Tolkien, Letters, op. cit., no. 256, to Colin Bailey, 1964.
26. Ibid., no. 91, to Christopher Tolkien, 1944.
27. Ibid., no. 165, to Houghton Mifflin, 1955.
28. J. R. R. Tolkien, Morgoth's Ring, op. cit., p. 311.
29. J. R. R. Tolkien, Letters, op. cit., no. 131, to Milton Waldman, 1951.
30. Humphrey Carpenter, op. cit., p. 98.
31. J. R. R. Tolkien, Letters, op. cit., no. 19, to Stanley Unwin, 1937.
32. Ibid., no. 131, to Milton Waldman, 1951.
33. J. R. R. Tolkien, Morgoth's Ring, op. cit., p. 311.
34. Ibid., p. 304.
35. Christopher Tolkien in J. R. R. Tolkien, Morgoth's Ring, op. cit., p. 328.
36. J. R. R. Tolkien, Morgoth's Ring, op. cit., p. 331.
37. Ibid., p. 329.
38. J. R. R. Tolkien, Letters, op. cit., no. 269, to W. H. Auden, 1965.
39. Christopher Tolkien in J. R. R. Tolkien, The Return of the Shadow, op. cit., p. 86.
40. Regina Doman, "RE: Tolkien Knew: No Salvation in Hobbits," op. cit.
41. Christopher Tolkien in J. R. R. Tolkien, The Return of the Shadow, op. cit., p. 26.
42. J. R. R. Tolkien, Letters, op. cit., no. 5, to Geoffrey B. Smith, 1916.

43. Ibid., no. 153, to Peter Hastings, 1954.

44. Ezekiel 3:17-21.

45. Tarkington, Some Old Portraits (New York: Doubleday, Doran & Company, 1939), p. x.

CHAPTER SEVEN: COMPELLING ALTERNATIVE VIEWS

1. Tarkington, Some Old Portraits, op. cit., p. xf.

2. David W. Cloud, "Tolkien and *The Lord Of The Rings*" Logos Resource Pages (Logos Communication Consortium, February 5, 2002). Oct. 21, 2002 [logosresourcepages.org/rings.htm].

3. Jacket notes to Bradley J. Birzer, J. R. R. Tolkien's Sanctifying Myth (Wilmington: Intercollegiate Studies Institute, 2002).

4. Bradley J. Birzer, "The Christian Gifts of J. R. R. Tolkien" (New Oxford Review 67.10, November 2001). Oct. 21, 2002 [www.newoxfordreview.org/nov01/bradleybirzer.html].

5. Jacket notes to Gareth Knight, The Magical World of J. R. R. Tolkien (Oceanside: Sun Chalice Books, 2001).

6. See Patrick Curry, Defending Middle-Earth: Tolkien, Myth and Modernity (Houndmills, Basingstoke: Palgrave Macmillan, 1997).

7. J. R. R. Tolkien, Morgoth's Ring, op. cit., p. 322.

8. J. R. R. Tolkien, Letters, op. cit., no. 154, to Naomi Mitchison, 1954.

9. Ibid., no. 160, to Rayner Unwin, 1955.

10. Garth Kemerling, "Humanism" A Dictionary of Philosophical Terms and Names (Philosophy Pages, 1997-2002). Oct. 21, 2002 [www.philosophy-pages.com/dy/h9.htm#huma].

11. Ralph Waldo Emerson, "Samuel Hoar" The Complete Works of Ralph Waldo Emerson Centenary Edition (Boston & New York: Houghton Mifflin and Company, 1903-1904), Vol. 10, p. 439.

12. Ralph Waldo Emerson, "Inspiration" The Complete Works op. cit., Vol. 8, p. 273.

13. Ralph Waldo Emerson, "Wealth" The Complete Works op. cit., Vol. 6, p. 114.

14. Ralph Waldo Emerson, "The Sovreignty of Ethics" The Complete Works op. cit., Vol. 10, p. 188.

15. Tom Shippey, Interview with Claire E. White "Talking Tolkien with Thomas Shippey" (The Internet Writing Journal 6.2, March 2002). Oct. 28 2002 [www.writerswrite.com/journal/mar02/shippey.htm].

16. Edmund Fuller, "The Lord of the Hobbits" Ed. Issacs and Zimbardo

    Tolkien and the Critics (Notre Dame: University of Notre Dame Press, 1968), p. 33.

17. Henry David Thoreau, "Economy" _Walden_ _The Thoreau Reader_ (Richard Lenat, 2001-2002), §9. Nov. 18, 2002 [eserver.org/thoreau/walden1a.html].

18. Matthew 12:42.

19. Romans 8:35.

20. Romans 8:36-39.

21. Proverbs 23:7, NASB.

22. Joseph Pearce, "True Myth," op. cit.

23. Jacket notes to Joseph Pearce, _Tolkien: Man and Myth_ (San Francisco: Ignatius Press, 2001).

24. Joseph Pearce, Interview "J. R. R. Tolkien's Take on the Truth" (_Zenit - The World Seen From Rome_ November 15, 2001). Oct. 21, 2002 [zenit.org/english].

25. Ibid.

26. Ibid.

27. Ibid.

28. Ibid.

29. Garth Kemerling, "Just War Theory" _A Dictionary of Philosophical Terms and Names_ (Philosophy Pages, 1997-2002). Nov. 7, 2002 [www.philosophypages.com/dy/j.htm#jusw].

30. Joseph Pearce, "J.R.R. Tolkien's Take on the Truth," op. cit.

31. Benjamin G. Kohl, "Humanism" (_Believe Religious Information Source_). Oct. 21, 2002 [mb-soft.com/believe/txn/chrishum.htm].

32. Ibid.

33. Ibid.

34. Ibid.

35. R. G. Clouse, "Christian Humanism" (_Believe Religious Information Source_) Oct. 21, 2002 [mb-soft.com/believe/txn/chrishum.htm].

36. Romans 1:19-20.

37. Thomas Aquinas, _The Summa Theologica of St. Thomas Aquinas_ Second and Revised Edition Fathers of the English Dominican Province, trans. (London: Burns Oates & Washbourne, 1920, Online Edition Kevin Knight, 2000), I-II, Question 93, Article 2. Oct. 21, 2002 [www.newadvent.org/summa/].

38. James J. Fox, "Natural Law" _The Catholic Encyclopedia_ Volume 9 (New York: Robert Appleton Company, 1910, Online Edition: Kevin Knight,

1999). Oct. 21, 2002 [www.newadvent.org/cathen/09076a.htm].

39. Vernon K. Robbins, "Salvation History" (Dictionary of Socio-Rhetorical Terms. Emory University, 1999). Oct. 21, 2002 [www.emory.edu/COL-LEGE/RELIGION/faculty/robbins/SRI/defns/s_defns.html].

40. Regina Doman [regina@veraprise.com], "RE: Your Help, Please" (Private e-mail message to Greg Wright, [hjlotr@hotmail.com] 20 June 2002).

41. Mark Eddy Smith, Tolkien's Ordinary Virtues: Exploring the Spiritual Themes of the Lord of the Rings (Downers Grove: Intervarsity Press, 2002), p. 11.

42. Ibid., p. 11f.

43. Jacket notes to Mark Eddy Smith, op. cit.

44. Ibid.

45. Mark Eddy Smith, op. cit., p. 139.

46. Ibid., p. 140.

47. Jacket notes to Kurt D. Bruner and Jim Ware, Finding God in The Lord of the Rings (Wheaton: Tyndale House Publishers, 2001).

48. Kurt D. Bruner, Interview with Bo Emerson "'Rings' Trilogy by Tolkien Blends Faith with Fantasy" (The Atlanta Journal and Constitution Dec. 15, 2001), p. B.1.

CHAPTER EIGHT: CONCLUSIONS: GOLD, OR JUST GLITTER?

1. J. R. R. Tolkien, The Fellowship of the Ring, op. cit., p.182.

2. G. K. Chesterton, The Defendant (London: J. M. Dent, 1901), p. 16.

3. J. R. R. Tolkien, The Tolkien Reader, op. cit., p. 74.

4. J. R. R. Tolkien, Morgoth's Ring, op. cit., p. 320.

5. Edmund Fuller, op. cit., p. 31.

6. James 4:17.

7. J. R. R. Tolkien, The Tolkien Reader, op. cit., p. 75.

8. G. K. Chesterton, op. cit., p. 13.

9. J. R. R. Tolkien, The Tolkien Reader, op. cit., p. 77.

10. Ephesians 3:20.

11. Romans 8:31.

12. Eugene Peterson, epigraph in Warren Wiersbe, Preaching and Teaching with Imagination: The Quest for Biblical Ministry (Wheaton: Victor Books - SP Publications, 1994), p. 22.

13. Ezekiel 34:8-12.

14. J. R. R. Tolkien, Letters, op. cit., no. 142, to Robert Murray, 1953.

15. Proverbs 3:5-7.
16. 1 Corinthians 14:15.
17. William H. Willimon, "This Culture is Overrated" (<u>Leadership Journal</u> 18.1, Winter 1997), p. 29.
18. Calvin Miller, <u>The Empowered Communicator</u> (Nashville: Broadman & Holman, 1994), p. 127.
19. Deborah Windes, "The Cost of Living in a Suburban Paradise" (<u>Books and Culture</u> 4.1, January/February 1998), p. 6.
20. Regina Doman, "RE: Next Installment," op. cit.
21. J. R. R. Tolkien, <u>Letters</u>, op. cit., no. 306, to Michael Tolkien, 1967.
22. Ibid., no. 153, to Peter Hastings, 1954.